Shaking the Feather Boa

Shaking the Feather Boa

Risky Business & Other Adventures

E.C. (Ted) Burton

Edited by Erica Burton

hancock house

ISBN 978-0-88839-609-9

Cataloging in Publication Data

Burton, Edward C. (Edward Cherry), 1931–
Shaking the feather boa : risky business & other adventures / E.C. (Ted) Burton ; edited by Erica Burton.

Includes index.
Also available in electronic format.
ISBN 978-0-88839-609-9

1. Burton, Edward C. (Edward Cherry), 1931–.
2. Lawyers—Ontario—Biography. I. Burton, Erica II. Title.
KE416.B87A3 2009 340.092 C2009-904698-9
KF345.Z9B87 2009

Printed in South Korea — PACOM

Editor: Theresa Laviolette
Production: Mia Hancock
Cover Design: Mia Hancock
Photography:All photographs courtesy of Erica Burton unless otherwise credited.
Front cover images: Erica Burton

We acknowledge the financial support of the Government of Canada through the Book Publishing Industry Development Program (BPIDP) for our publishing activities.

Published simultaneously in Canada and the United States by

HANCOCK HOUSE PUBLISHERS LTD.
19313 Zero Avenue, Surrey, B.C. Canada V3S 9R9
(604) 538-1114 Fax (604) 538-2262

HANCOCK HOUSE PUBLISHERS
1431 Harrison Avenue, Blaine, WA U.S.A. 98230-5005
(604) 538-1114 Fax (604) 538-2262

***Website:* www.hancockhouse.com**
***Email:* sales@hancockhouse.com**

Contents

Introduction

In the days of my youth, that is to say, before I turned sixty, I measured my age in terms of the passage of time. Looking back on it, though, I now believe it to be more appropriate to measure my age in terms of the adventures I had along the way. These were real nerve tingling adventures on a par with anything that ever happened to Tom Sawyer and Huck Finn. Now that I am well into the decade past seventy my view is still developing and I must give due credit to the notion that the really important aspect of my life is the people who were with me on the voyage, my fellow travelers, so to speak. And I am prepared to concede that there can be satisfaction in intellectual accomplishment, as well as from friends, which is quite an admission from a dedicated hedonist.

Even with the passage of time, as I remember my adventures I recollect the thrill and apprehension of the moment. I have always thought of them as "shaking the feather boa." It is an expression that has come down on my mother's side of the family, and even my grown children will talk about shaking the feather boa when they are describing some daredevil or risky venture. This is how it came into the family vocabulary.

Back in the Gay Nineties, fashionable ladies often wore a long snake-like scarf of feathers when they wanted to dress up to go out in public. The fashion was going out of favor when my mother was born in 1905, but someone had stored one of those old feather boas in a trunk in a dusty corner of the attic of the family home in the sleepy, rural South. As a little girl, when she was bored, she would wait till everyone was out of the house, sneak up to the second floor, and pull on the rope that let the attic stairs down. In the far corner of the attic, under the dusty window, she would open the steamer trunk. Right on the very top was a feather boa, a horrid black and gray thing that to a child looked just like a real boa constrictor. With her heart beating madly she would grab the loathsome thing by one end and shake it furiously, causing it to undulate along its length, stirring up clouds of dust. A few moments of this and she would be convinced that it was a real live snake. Shrieking with fear and delight she would slam the trunk lid down and flee the attic, quivering with excitement.

Mom scared the bejesus out of herself every time she did this, and her brother and older sisters admired her for her feats of bravery. She always felt good after shaking the feather boa. I, too, always felt good after a hair-raising adventure, and I guess I still do, although real adrenaline-pumping adventures don't seem to come my way any more.

I had an extremely interesting childhood, which makes it easy to remember my early days. Most of it was spent in Canada, although a substantial amount of it was spent in the USA. I had more travel and adventure by the time I was twelve than most people have in a lifetime. Indeed, I had a full and interesting adulthood, although not nearly so exciting as my childhood. Simply put, there are many positive landmarks in my life at all stages to facilitate and reinforce my memory. I think of these landmarks as milestones.

Both Mom and Pop were great reminiscers and raconteurs. Their tales of what had gone before never bored me. Many a pleasant evening would begin by one or the other of my parents saying, as we did the dishes by the light of a hissing Coleman lamp, "Teddy, do you remember the time your dog Rickey was bitten by a rattlesnake at The Grove?" Rickey was my constant companion for years of my childhood and traveled with us everywhere. How could I forget him? How could I forget Hickory Glen Grove, where my uncle, The Reverend T.H. McConnell, played werewolf with my cousin Betty Wells and myself?

The most important aid to my memory is something everyone who has been seriously ill or injured will understand. In May of 1996 I had a stroke. It knocked me flat, but after a few days I was able to move around. I kept improving for about a year, but then I plateaued, and I am only just now, in 2002, beginning to get a good night's sleep. I often lie half awake and think for hours every night. As I lie in that state between waking and sleeping, I dream. I re-live exciting episodes in my life. Interesting memories float up, like little specks floating around in a well. As I look into the well a flicker of movement catches my eye, becoming clearer as it drifts into a shaft of sunlight. It is a water spider, white and groping because it has never before seen daylight.

It is like that with my early memories. If I contemplate them over a period of time they rise up to the surface where I can inspect them in detail. If I happen to be sleeping in my armchair, I can flick on the light and make a note for future reference. If it is an interesting episode and I can get to it within two or three days, I will write it up.

Now, looking down into the well of my memory I see what appears to be a bright metal speck. I lose it for a moment, and then it re-appears in a shaft of light, twisting and turning like a falling leaf. Little by little the speck enlarges and becomes clear. It is a Hamilton Metal Plane, on floats. I see it heeled up on a beach, twanging ropes restraining it from flying in the high wind that assails it. I vaguely recall seeing it that way once on a beach in Red Lake. I would have been nine years old at the time. Quite plainly I see where the aluminum paint has flaked off the surface of the wing, leaving bare streaks down the tops of the ridges of the corrugations.

As I contemplate the scene, time advances and I am a boy of about twelve at Orient Bay at the south end of Lake Nipigon. I hear the rather discordant sound of the wind blowing over the corrugated skin of the Hamilton. I remark to myself that it is different from the sound the wind makes on a fabric-covered aircraft. I think it over for a few days, and decide that the scene at the dock and the adventure that went with it is worth writing up. That is how the chapter called "A Ride In The Hamilton" came into being, as well as many of the other anecdotes in the book. They are as factual as I can make them. There were very few blanks that had to be filled in from imagination, even half a century later.

The really interesting thing about my early life is not that it was hard and that I had to fight my way to the top, but quite the opposite. The fact is that I had a tremendous amount of help from well-meaning relatives and associates all the way. The way to the top of the mountain was an uphill slope, made easier to climb by the many good people I met along the way.

The people, aside from my parents and relatives who had the most influence on me in my early years, were the Traves family of Oakville, and Bill and Doris Davis of Amos and points north. These two couples were very fine people who had been friends of my parents since before I was born, but I can't really say a great deal about them at this distance, other than that they were instrumental in my humanizing.

Yes, humanizing. It's what friends and relatives do for children that make it possible for others to live with them. It's the obligation people have towards their friends' and neighbors' children.

Like the time at Amos, Quebec when I slipped and broke my arm when I was five years old; the local hospital would not admit me for reasons better left unspoken in the interest of religious harmony. A meeting of friends was convened to decide what to do about me, and I was in dreadful agony. Bill Davis pulled me over to him, letting me bury my face in the polar bear and wolverine fur of his winter parka, which was the badge of northern pilots. That way no one could see me cry. Or perhaps they just pretended not to be able to see. As I said elsewhere, I was extraordinarily fortunate in the people I met up with during my formative years.

Or like the time in Toronto when I had to have a tonsillectomy, and John and Nancy Traves allowed the operation to take place on their dining room table. We lived with them while I recuperated, and on several other occasions during my very young years.

Wedding day, July 30, 1960.

I met Erica a day or two after I returned to Kenora from law school in the spring of 1959. She was working for Magistrate J.V. Fregeau as his court reporter. He did not like me very well at first, but we later became very good friends, in spite of the fact that he had advised her not to marry me "because he has been in the bush too long." However, heedless of this advice, Erica and I were married in a little white clapboard church on a quiet street in Kenora in 1960. Our families and friends were immensely pleased with us. In due course we had three children, with whom we are good friends, and the family has grown to include their spouses and children. I wonder if children help their fathers grow up, or do they merely wait around as spectators while it is happening?

As you might expect I have written and done very little of a creative nature that Erica did not assist me with in one way or another. I have to admit that she helped me to grow up, an exercise I have not yet quite finished, even though I can see the end of the line. She, of course, is the chief of the interesting people that the Creator has put in my path for my benefit. She is a smart lady. Without her assistance and encouragement this book would not have come into being. I dedicate this book to her.

I must also acknowledge the assistance of my friend of sixty years, Bill Agnew, who for years was the smartest kid in school in Sault Ste Marie, and who contributed greatly to bringing some order and cohesion to this manuscript. And I am also grateful for the help of Charlie Wilkins, an accomplished author who makes his home in Thunder Bay and freely gives encouragement and advice to aspiring writers. Many others have been instrumental in bringing this manuscript to life. Some of them figure in the stories that follow.

01: Antecedents

The novelist Graham Greene once wrote that there is always one moment in childhood when the door opens and lets the future in. I think that in my case there were many such moments. Some were just a few seconds long, and some were days long, but they mostly all occurred in association with interesting people. Not necessarily good people, but interesting nonetheless. It is to the interesting people in my life that I owe the most, beginning with my mother and father.

My parents, Ed and Lucille Burton, were really fine folks, as were all their friends. I was truly fortunate in most of the adults who impinged on me in my early life. They couldn't always read very well, and I know that some of them couldn't sign their own names on their paychecks. On the other hand there were many teachers, engineers, pilots, adventurers, explorers, lawyers, politicians, and writers in their number, and I found something to admire in all of them, even the clergymen, whom I liked individually, if not as a breed. Collectively all these people, even the illiterates, guided me through the tight spots, as opposed to squeezing me through like a block of metal being extruded through a die. I was extraordinarily fortunate to find myself in the company of kind and reasonable adults at times when I was about to make a colossal fool of myself, or about to do something really hurtful to someone, perhaps even myself. As a matter of fact, I believe most of the people I rubbed shoulders with all my life were kind and reasonable. And many of them liked to shake the feather boa once in a while.

My childhood and youthful experiences have left me with the belief that in a civilized society there is a duty on people to take some responsibility for young people outside their own immediate family circle. Many people other than my parents either beat me about the head and ears, or were very good to me, and I am probably a better person for it.

The structure of my life was cast on an ocean liner in December 1927, when my father, Edward Cherry Burton, known to all as Eddie, met my mother, Lucille Emma Tervin, known as Cile, at an afternoon tea dance in one of the ship's lounges. Pop, for that was what I always called him, was a dashing, but somewhat battered Englishman. On this occasion he was returning from England, where he had gone to consult doctors to see if anything further could be done for injuries sustained in a terrible airplane crash in 1924 in Northwestern Ontario. Mom and her sister, Cuthill, were homeward bound for Florida from a European holiday. As Mom told it, she was quite pleasantly surprised when Pop came lurching through the chairs, swinging his cane, frightening old ladies, and taking her hand, while the band played ragtime.

Pop returned to take on various flying jobs in Canada and, after a courtship by correspondence, just before Christmas in 1929 he boarded a train for Florida. They were married on New Year's Eve by Aunt Cuthill's husband, Dr. Mac, of the First Presbyterian Church, in Daytona Beach, Florida.

Dr. Mac (The Reverend Dr. T.H. McConnell) figured largely in the lives of my cousin Betty Wells Nelson and me while we were growing up. He had a small, but fashionable, Presbyterian church in Orlando, and a ramshackle country home on a forty-acre orange grove nearby that was always full of relatives during the depression. At various times when Pop was off on some flying expedition, my mother and I would spend time at The Grove, and occasionally Pop joined us, and the rest of the clan, at the family compound.

Pop was flying the airmail out of Toronto when I came along on the seventh day of December 1931. The family was living high off the hog, sporting a Packard car and a daily maid.

Just a few days after I was born, Pop made a night parachute jump from his Stearman Speedmail when the weather closed in around him. Following an uneasy descent, during which he had good reason to wonder if he might be falling into Lake Erie, he landed safely in a farmer's field near Dunville, just west of Hamilton. The aircraft landed, more or less intact, a couple of miles away, and most of the cargo was salvaged — but the Stearman burned when searchers accidentally tripped a flare. It was the first forced night jump by a civilian in Canada. The Irving Chute Company gave him a ruby-eyed gold caterpillar (they being the critters that make the silk used in parachutes) that I still have.

Pop became the darling of the press because of this and other exploits. Always reticent, as you would expect a proper Englishman to be, he never capitalized on his popular acclaim. Pilots, because of the nature of their game, have a lot of time when they are doing nothing, or at any rate they did when aviation was young. They had hours and hours of sit-

With father, Eddie.

About age four.

ting up on their noisy, vibrating platforms with only a compass and an oil pressure gauge to watch. In the evening they swatted mosquitoes in their tents or sat in dingy hotel rooms with only yesterday's newspaper for company. Many of them drank, which seemed to be a curse on pilots in the early days.

But not Pop. He read widely, and wrote marvelous letters, and sketched. Many of the letters and sketches have survived in the bottom of steamer trunks and in boxes of moth-eaten blankets that should have been tossed out half a century ago. But you know how it is with pack rats. As I grew older, many letters and sketches were created with me in mind. They are of events and scenes which he knew would interest me, such as my dog Rickey riding on a horse-drawn sleigh back at the Perron Mines; my little friends in Ottawa sliding on the banks of a canal; the frozen cream at the top of a glass milk bottle (long before homogenization and square wax paper cartons) pushing the cardboard lid up like a little cap. Kids and dogs liked to sneak up on the neighbor's porch and swipe the blob of frozen cream. These are the sights of an era long gone, and I will always remember them because of the sketches.

Mom was not just an appendage of my father. She, and three of her

With mother, Lucille, shopping in Daytona Beach

The Rev. "Mac" and Cuthill MacConnell.

four sisters and a brother, all got university degrees. She got her teaching degree from Florida State University at Tallahassee on a scholarship, which required her to teach for two years, so she moved to Daytona Beach to be with her sisters, Pauline and Cuthill, who were both teaching high school. Mom loathed and detested teaching, so when the opportunity to go to the *St. Augustine Herald* as a reporter presented itself, she jumped at it, paying back one-half of her scholarship rather than teaching a second year. When she had paid off her debts she and her sister Cuthill took a pleasure cruise to Europe; but I have already told you what happened on that trip.

Aside from that first year of teaching, she only entered a schoolroom once more, to teach evening adult education classes at the Whitedog Reserve on the Winnipeg River, north of Kenora. This was after my father died in 1966, and she needed something to do. She liked the people she dealt with, and the rough characters among them politely refrained from trying to murder her even while beating and stabbing each other, but the experience confirmed to her that she was not cut out to be a teacher. She turned her hand to other endeavors, including writing for and editing a small-town newspaper.

DeFuniak Springs, Florida, mother's home town.

Mom was born in 1905 and raised in DeFuniak Springs, a sleepy little town in north Florida built around a perfectly round body of water exactly one mile in circumference, which is supposed to bestow everlasting life on you if you drink enough of it. Local wisdom had it that the lake was connected to Ponce de Leon Springs some miles away, and other cold, deep, life-giving lakes, by underground caverns.

My mother's relatives in the South were good folks who loved me dearly and who had great influence on me, more so than my dad's relatives. The patriarch was Franklin Quitman Tervin, my mother's father, who raised six children and supported an assortment of in-laws, and they say he never spent a nickel on himself.

Grandfather Quitman Tervin was universally loved and respected by both whites and blacks. He ran sawmills in the piney woods between Pensacola and Tallahassee, settling his employees and other hangers-on in little scratched-up towns in the back woods. (Among his hangers-on was Jacqueline Cochran, a little girl with no visible parents, who became a famous aviatrix of the 1920s and 1930s.) I barely remember him as a

The Orlando, Florida school that I attended sporadically when staying at The Grove.

craggy old man who rode children on his shoulders, but I do remember the pleasant ripples it caused in rural Walton County black homes when it was announced that the young man at the door seeking to buy moonshine was the grandson of Quit Tervin.

Grandfather Tervin was raised in the little town of Freeport, once a pirate stronghold, but today a comfortable, sleepy village on the edge of the bayou. With the lumber from his sawmills deep in the piney woods he built houses in DeFuniak Springs and other towns on the Florida panhandle. Many of these houses, built from heartwood selected by him, still stand.

My grandmother, Mamie Baker Tervin, was part Isle of Skye, and part Huguenot, coming to DeFuniak Springs from Carolina in the 1870s with her father and sister. Her family always called her Mother Mamie. When she thought we were ill, she would put my cousin Betty Wells and me to bed with mustard plasters, feeding us spoonfuls of sugar laced with turpentine. I suppose it was good for us, though it tasted dreadful.

Mother Mamie's father was The Reverend Robert Quarterman Baker, an ironclad Presbyterian from North Carolina who had started out as an officer with the army of the Confederacy, but ended up in the church because of what he had seen in the terrible Civil War battles. One must remember that they were able to blow human beings apart with remarkable efficiency, but they had no anesthetics and the germ theory had not yet been developed. When I was a kid in the 1930s, small-town USA had many dreadfully decrepit old men with no legs who got around on little wheeled platforms that they pushed with leather-padded hands. My mother remembered her grandfather Baker sitting in his rocker in his declining years, still contemplating the morality of the war, shaking his head and mumbling, "We thought we were right, we thought we were right."

It is possible, barely possible, that there is a drop of Creek Indian blood in the family lineage. My mother believed it was so, but her sisters did not. During the 1800s there was a very fine Indian chief in Northwest Florida named Sam Storey, and I would be pleased to think his people might have been among my ancestors. My personal observations are that North American Indians have many strong attributes, among them a willingness to share, and the ability to accept other people as they are without trying to change them. My reading would be that this was true in the early days of settlement of North Florida. Perhaps some of these traits devolved to me.

My father's origins were in England. His father, Captain George Burton, an Extra Master, had considerable influence on me, although I never met him. He was the stuff of legend, being a multi-faceted person who designed and supervised the building of ships, wrote navigation treatises, and opened the trade lanes with Brazil. It's all there in yellowed newspaper clippings that survived through the decades. After seeing the transition from sail to steam, he retired, but returned to sea as Master of Cadets on the square-rigged clipper ship *Port Jackson* for one last voyage to Australia. My dad held him in high esteem, and so do I, even if it is a century later.

Captain George's first wife, my grandmother, died when Pop was still very young, leaving him to be raised by a benevolent stepmother of whom he was very fond. My biological grandmother had pukah sahib antecedents by the names of Cherry and Padwick who were colonels and judge advocate generals in Madras, and that sort of thing, their offspring tending to marry within their class. Their class, by the way, was English middle class, which was an aristocracy of competence having its origins

Grandfather, Captain George Burton.

The *Port Jackson,* built in 1882, under full sail.

in the latter part of the 19th century. They were reasonably well off by the standards of the day but worked for everything they had, unlike the people who fancied themselves to be "upper class."

As I step back and attempt to contemplate my ancestors with detachment it strikes me that there were many doers of deeds and people of accomplishment among them. It causes me to wonder if a love of adventure and a desire to stretch one's self is a hereditary trait. Modesty not being one of my strengths, I will permit myself to say that I somehow acquired the will to do something of value. Unfortunately I never acquired the knack of making money, although in my declining years I continue to try to push the envelope, even though there is no reward in sight. It may sound sanctimonious to say that I feel an obligation to share some of what I learned in the last seventy years even if I don't get paid for it.

If it does, I will offset it by stating that the famous villain of the boudoir, explorer, swordsman, anthropologist, linguist, and writer, Sir Richard Burton, (he translated unexpurgated versions of *The Perfumed Garden, The Kama Sutra,* and *The Arabian Nights*) was a distant cousin of the family, or so one of his biographers implied. Pop refused to discuss with me the possibility of kinship to Sir Richard, leading me to believe that it was very likely so, just like the hint of family relationship to Chief Sam Storey on my mother's side. Anyway, Sir Richard was a scalawag, and one of the more flamboyant people of his time, so he couldn't have been all bad. If I am related to him, so much the better, as it adds something spicy to the bland English blood I inherited — a leavening influence, so to speak. Mind, there is nothing wrong with good, solid English genes once you get by the fact that the English can be so damned proper.

Not all my dad's relatives were stuffy. The Gartshores in Toronto, for example, were fine people who took my father into the family bosom while he was recuperating from his airplane crash in 1924. Their Spitfire flyer son, Boyd, and his beautiful wife, Marnie, were the type of people they made inspirational war movies about during the 1940s.

Being half a world away, I did not get to know most of my father's relatives. One of his brothers, Uncle Charlie, was a chicken farmer near Stoney Creek in Southern Ontario. We were not congenial, as most of our relationship consisted in his trying to persuade me that sin came in a bottle — a proposition totally unacceptable to a young man raised in the bush in the 1950s. Pop's other brother, my Uncle Willie, was a well-known Pentecostal missionary in Darkest Africa. Willie was, by all accounts, devoted to the ministry and well intentioned in his efforts to make converts and dispense salvation. He sent tracts to me, but they were no more effective in weaning me away from sin than were Charlie's blandishments. Both Charlie and Willie meant well, but they simply were not equipped to deal with a young North American lad who had laughter and fun in his makeup. Pop also had two sisters, Freda and Gracie, but I only ever met Freda.

In the summer of 1955, Uncles Willie and Charlie had come to our big house at the provincial air base on Coney Island in Kenora, for an extended visit. With them they brought Aunt Freda, all the way from England, hoping to dry her out. They were pretty stiff-necked about it, so she huddled up with me for protection. By sticking together, and with occasional help from my father, we were able to fend off the sanctimonious brethren. I should mention that Willie had won a considerable measure of fame, if not fortune, as a Pentecostal minister, but he had done very well indeed as an artist in oils and watercolors, and had authored a number of books about African customs and missionary work.

Our summer neighbors, the Horans, the Hollands, and the Browns, were all good two-fisted social drinkers. They knew that Uncle Willie was death on grog, and out of deference to him (they didn't care much for

The three Burton brothers, Eddie, Willie, Charlie, Kenora 1955.

Uncle Charlie) they vowed not to drink so much as a drop of alcohol all summer. As far as I know they didn't, either. But my dad, who was a person of moderation, was sixty-four and tired. He liked a little nip after a long day in the air, but my mother would not let him have it in the house. He kept a bottle of rye under the washing machine on the back porch, out of sight of his brothers and the neighbors. After the day's flying was over he would lean watchfully on the doorjamb while he refreshed himself. Our neighbors were furious when they found he was breaking the taboo on booze, but being of saintly disposition they refrained from partaking until Willie had departed.

The truth is that Pop was not really an ally of his brothers in their zeal to reform the world. Screwing up his face, he would pretend to go to sleep whenever Charlie was talking, and he would pretend to be deaf when Willie was talking.

As soon as he was off the train on the occasion of the momentous, but dry, visit, Uncle Willie was pre-empted by the local Pentecostal church to conduct a service every evening. I suppose it was churlish of me, but I

Family home on Coney Island, c. 1950.

refused to go to these evening meetings, preferring to take my Aunt Freda over to town for a beer. However, one evening before he left, Willie dragooned my friend Bob Campbell and me and my parents into attending at the little local Pentecostal assembly place. The service was predictably fundamentalist until the very end, or what should have been the end. Some sixth sense, some instinct for self-preservation, warned Pop and Bob that mischief was afoot, causing them to rise and make a mad dash for the door. They escaped a bare nanosecond before one of the faithful slammed and locked the door. Trying to follow them was pointless. My mother pulled me back down into my seat.

What happened next is almost too bizarre to imagine. Suddenly, and without warning, the congregation metamorphosed into a swirling, chanting mass of people who seemed to be without individual wills, led in their mindless ecstasy by the charismatic young local parson. By twos and threes they wobbled to the front, eventually forming a mob of thirty or forty people, all churning about and laying their hands on a blind man, exhorting the Lord to cure him. I don't think the Lord was favorably impressed, because the next time I saw the man he was still blind.

While all this was going on I sat huddled up with my mother, who was rigid with distaste. The chanting rolled over the little church like a

With my cousin, Betty Wells Nelson.

hypnotic wave. Hearing a noise behind me, I looked around and saw an old lady lying out on the seat, going into spasms and making unintelligible noises. Apparently she was a mite too feeble to join the others in the laying on of hands, so she had her own little service on the seat, speaking in tongues, the better to get the Lord's attention. To give Uncle Willie his due, I don't think he approved of the direction in which the service was moving. Hovering around the seething blob of people, he attempted to exert a calming influence, saying something to the effect that he was sure Brother So-and-So would be much improved now.

The day Willie and Charlie left was not altogether a happy one in spite of the crimp they had put in the neighborhood activities. Willie radiated goodness, and Charlie was exceedingly kind and generous, even to me. Some days after Willie left Kenora, another witness to the spectacle at the church told me that Willie had asked him to convey to me that he was sorry he had asked me to that particular service, and that I should not judge him or his religion on the basis of the laying-on-of-hands incident.

Now, you may think that I am being harsh and disloyal in my portrayal of family members and their strongly held beliefs. I don't think so. I have merely called it as I saw it, and what I saw in that little church was a demonstration of mass hypnosis and mass hysteria that I cannot believe was related to religion. If anything, the episode confirmed my rather negative view of organized religion. My mother's brother-in-law, Dr. Mac, detected this negative attitude when I was still quite young and, while he did not encourage it, he did nothing to persuade me or humbug me out of it. For example, he decreed that I should not be forced to memorize the catechism like every other child baptized in the Presbyterian Church. My dear cousin and soul mate, Betty Wells, was required to memorize it and spout it back publicly, but I was exempted, which made her furious. I certainly am grateful for Dr. Mac's foresight and understanding.

It would not be quite accurate to say I am proud of my ancestry, as in my view the concept of pride should reside in something worthwhile that one accomplishes by his own effort, and not because of something bestowed on one by accident, or the efforts of other people. It would, however, be accurate and truthful to say that I am immensely pleased by the genes the Creator bestowed on me, whatever their origins, as these genes come from people who were doers, not drones, on both sides of the family.

02: Milestones

Some people view life as a continuity of events that merge into each other, in which individual events do not assume great importance. Perhaps nothing memorable ever happened to them. I tend to lean the other way, believing that one grows and lives a life by fits and starts, which may be likened to milestones along the way. The events that are the milestones may be creditable or discreditable, and the experience of them shapes us for better or worse.

Everyone has, I suppose, done things they are ashamed of, but it is not good to introspect too much on one's stupidities and wickedness, and certainly not to put them in writing for all the world to see, as the fine line between confessing and bragging often becomes blurred.

Memory is fallible and, as I have already said, I admit to filling in the blanks with information told to me by others, particularly older family members, at least in the early stages of my life. Looking back over the events I am frequently astounded by what happened, but every one of these things really did happen when I was growing up just about as I relate them here.

The 1930s and 40s were really a great time for a kid who was part of a mobile family and whose parents were not afraid to let him try his wings. Such a time may never come around again, not with the tendency of modern government to control everything we do in order to keep us safe from harm. Not in the stifling atmosphere of the politically correct. Not in the era of sanitized, bland human endeavor from which "Mama State" has removed all the spice. And my descendants will be the poorer for it.

Of course there were many milestones in my life, but these are some of the childhood milestones I remember best.

Age Three – The Rattlesnake

Children don't seem to have an instinctive fear of snakes, but it doesn't take them long to learn. I hate 'em now, as an adult, and I remember how I learned my revulsion.

With my doting relatives at Daytona Beach.

The Great Depression was at its worst, so various members of my mother's extended family retreated to an orange grove in Florida that was owned by generous-hearted Dr. Mac, the husband of my mother's sister Cuthill. Hickory Glen Grove was on a little lake the family called Lake Dot, which was then in the country outside Orlando, but is now within the city limits. Over the years the grove was a haven when there were no flying jobs available for my dad, or when he was off on an expedition.

My lovely tomboy cousin Betty Wells and I amused ourselves by playing stick ball, reading, chasing chickens, swimming in the lake, playing werewolf with Dr. Mac, and just basking in the bosom of our family. Occasionally an adult would help us raise a sheet in the rowboat and we would sail clumsily around the lake. The boat was normally tied by the bow to a plank just above the water level, which skirted a rickety stage on which assorted aunts and female visitors liked to sun themselves in their birthday suits.

One unexpectedly warm day in winter I was playing on the plank, while several women of the family were sunbathing on the upper stage. Unnoticed by anyone, a huge diamondback rattler slithered onto the plank, probably from the rowboat that was touching the shore at the stern. Like the rest of us, the snake was basking in the sun. Perhaps it did not notice me at first, either. When I saw the critter I was interested in it, but probably not frightened of it. I drew it to the attention of my guardians on the upper platform.

An electric hush filled the air. An aunt whispered, "Teddy, stay absolutely still. Don't go near it. Cile, keep talking to him while I run up and get Dr.

Mac and his gun." With that she crept quietly to shore, trying not to shake the staging and thereby alarming the snake, which by now was coiled within striking distance of the foot of the ladder that led to the upper deck.

My admittedly rather patchy memory takes over at this point, and the tales told by the family fireside in childhood recede in importance as the building blocks of the narrative. I don't pretend to know when childhood memories achieve continuity and accuracy, but I assume everyone has a first memory of some singular event that took place when they were three, or four, or five. This is my memory of an early astonishing event. I must have been three or four.

I stood on the outer end of the plank while my mother spoke quietly to me. There was a compelling urgency in her voice as she told me to remain still. I began to be afraid of the rattler that, almost seventy years later, I remember as huge. It simply remained in one place, all coiled up, its head weaving rhythmically as it contemplated me with tiny, beady eyes that stared, unblinking and hypnotic. The sun shone on its bright scales, making it appear wet. Occasionally its tail quivered, giving out a dry rattle. I became rooted to the plank in terror.

Eons later, perhaps five minutes, Dr. Mac appeared with his big 12-gauge pump gun in his hands, feeding shells into the magazine as he ran. Like everyone else on that milestone day, he was starkers. He advanced on the stage until it began to vibrate. The snake became alarmed, looking around for the source of the movement. The waving of its head became quicker, more erratic. It was perhaps eight feet away from me and could have reached me in one or two seconds.

Dr. Mac brought the big gun up to his shoulder and blew the snake's head off. The body thrashed on the plank then fell into the shallows, still twitching. I was astonished by the sudden appearance of a ragged, oblong hole in the plank, white around the edges where the fresh wood showed.

I climbed the ladder to the circle of protective arms, and the term "family bosom" took on tangible meaning, as six or eight of them were smothering me all at once. To this very day I hold female bosoms in great esteem, and I do not sneer at the great American "tit culture." Towels were handed around and the adults' modesty was restored.

That's all. Memory turns off there. I suppose we all went up to the screened veranda and had lemonade.

What is a memory for if it doesn't teach you anything? Perhaps nothing. But, aside from developing a profound affection for the female bosom, the snake incident taught me several other things I will never forget. I learned not to mess with diamondback rattlers. I learned that 12-bore guns make a hell of a lot of noise, can do a lot of damage, and can be mighty useful in certain circumstances. To this very day I value these early lessons.

When I turned thirteen, Dr. Mac gave me the big old Winchester Model 12 shotgun and a little "Saturday Night Special" revolver. I had them both until a disgruntled policeman took the revolver away from me and a careless gunsmith lost the shotgun.

Age Six – An Early Snow

By the time one is six years of age one begins to think in abstract terms, and a sense of values develops. Subsequent memories of this time are not by any means complete, but in later life one may recall how incidents fit into the whole picture.

At six I was aware that the two airplanes tied up on the banks of the Harricanaw River at Amos in Northern Quebec were very important to the well being of my family, and to my father's employer, Bill Davis, who owned the airplanes. Amos Airways, he called his business. I don't suppose I knew much about money, or earning a living, but I knew my father loved the Fairchild FC 2 and the Curtiss Robin. Occasionally I went with him on one of his trips, and I became aware that he actually liked to fly the machines. All his life he seemed to grow in stature when he was in command of an aircraft. More than that, he had to fly them. They were central to his life, and keeping them in the air was an important endeavor to which even a six year old could contribute, if only by bringing his dad his slippers when he was tired.

And so it was when the call came one fall night in 1937 or so, that every man associated with the flying business in Amos rushed down to the river, for the planes were sinking under the weight of an unseasonable wet snow. Every man and one kid — me. All down the shore, lights flashed and disembodied voices drifted through the snow-filled night as the people associated with the various flying services frantically swept the wings of their machines.

Pop ordered me very firmly to stay out of the way and wait in the shack that served as office, waiting room, warehouse, and workshop. But it wasn't long before he, or Bill, called to me to bring a rope, and I was pleased to do it. It made me feel really useful. A few minutes later I answered the phone when no adult was around to do it. "Amos Airways," I squeaked, putting as much authority into my voice as was possible. Then Bill asked me to damp down the wood stove, thereby saving him a trip from the dock to the office.

I sensed that the men were beginning to appreciate my contribution to the exercise. It is a wonderful thing for a kid to realize that he is an individual human being with value that goes beyond his place in the family circle. I was fortunate to come to that realization in the space of a couple of hours that night on the banks of the Harricanaw River. I don't suppose I philosophized about it at the time, but something good came out of the exercise that was over and above the fun of the moment.

And then the supreme honor was bestowed on me. Someone handed me a broom and assigned me to the tail feathers of one of the airplanes. All my responsibility! If I didn't do it the airplane could sink by the tail. Of course I did it, and the men kept the wings clear. Every hour or so they would turn the machines so that the other side was next to the dock, and the sweeping would start again.

When the storm abated, Amos Airways was still in business. My relationship with adults changed noticeably. It was at this time that adults stopped cautioning me whenever I went on the dock or put my hand on a strut. A milestone! I am sure my improved status had something to do with the night of the early snow.

From this experience I learned that if you work hard at a difficult job a reward will probably come to you somewhere down the line, in this case the reward being the newfound confidence and respect adults felt for me. And I learned not to beat on cold aircraft fabric with a sweeping broom, as it will cause ringworm in the spring, a phenomenon that sixty-five years later is still not understood by a surprising number of people who fly fabric covered airplanes in winter.

Once again a door had opened and let the future in.

Ages Seven to Eleven – Vignettes

Nothing leaps out at me that I remember as being an unmistakable milestone during these years. Undoubtedly there were such, as we lived in Florida, Quebec, and many places in Ontario during this period, often uprooting four or five times in one year. Little episodes come to mind, but

Favorite pastime: going flying, here in a Vickers Vedette.

not the small, intense epics that I would call milestones. Perhaps just surviving this time of my life was a milestone in itself. Even as I write, unconnected little memories come flooding back.

Like the time I stood by my mother on the deck of a steamer in New York harbor. My attention was about equally divided between looking at the USS *Ranger,* then the largest aircraft carrier in the world, and observing the consternation caused by my dog, Rickey, who was peeing gallons on the freshly scrubbed planks. Fade out.

Or the time I crawled out of the front hold of the Vickers Vedette flying boat during a fuel stop at Wawa, on the north shore of Lake Superior. I desperately wanted a private patch of bush to lie down in and recover my equilibrium, a place where not even my mother would know how sick I was. She was pretty sick herself, and didn't need me on her hands. When I looked up from the ground there was a circle of curious children around me,

The Red Lake Forestry Base, 1940s.

just watching. A girl about my own age made all the others go away, and when the aircraft was gassed and ready she called me to get up. Fade out.

Sleeping in a Murphy bed with Peter Traves at the Windsor Arms Hotel in Toronto, when the house we lived in was under quarantine during a measles epidemic. Driving our fathers crazy by banging the bed up into its vertical position in the middle of the night. Fade out.

Paddling across Skookum Creek with another boy and an old man in the night. It was how you had to travel from Red Lake to Forestry Point where we lived, unless you had a boat, as there was no road. Fade out.

I must have been nine that summer, and I remember a great deal of it.

I remember Hoofer, the dog who walked on the stumps of his legs, his paws having been frozen off the previous winter.

I remember Andy, the short, fat little cook at the fire ranger's cookery. He would put an apron on and light the stove before he got dressed. We kids at the base would get up early, early, and peek through the screen door at the spectacle of the fire lighting. Andy's "nuggies" seemed to nearly touch the floor when he spread his legs and bent over to light the birch bark in the ash pan under the firebox. Gross! Fascinating! But, more fascinating than gross.

I remember opening my grade four correspondence courses in the fall, and being furious at being forced to get an education. I failed grade four, but next year I skipped grade five. There must be a milestone here,

Forestry boat *Ranger* and a Norseman at Orient Bay OPAS base.

even if I can't recognize it. Until the day I left law school, I never did learn to be comfortable in the dunghill of education.

And still later, in the fall flying over Lake Superior in a Stinson Reliant, imploring my father to land. I was often airsick as a child. He brought the machine down to wave-top height so that I could see for myself why a landing was impossible.

And next summer, boom running with boys from the reserve at the sawmill just outside Fort Frances. Men would come out to chase us off, but we were so light we just skimmed over the logs in our bare feet, and the heavier men couldn't catch us.

And patching up a freight canoe with tar, and hovering in it beside the dock, where I could watch my father and a policeman unload the body of a man who had been killed by a bear, and getting a licking for it because he had told me to stay away from the dock before he left to retrieve the body. The view of the body was worth the licking, but ever afterwards I have been very nervous about bears. I tend to give them a wide berth.

I had a lot to do with boats as a young fellow. I was partial to both boats and airplanes, and with secret encouragement from Pop's friends, I learned how to handle aircraft in straight and level flight; but that was a far cry from actually being able to call myself a pilot (I was thirty years old before I got my pilots license). However, they didn't let kids fly airplanes. So, during my youth I had to get my adrenaline rush in boats.

I well remember a time at the Orient Bay base of the Provincial Air Service when I was twelve or thirteen. My mother and I were making a night crossing by boat from MacDiarmid to our home. We had a live chicken I had somehow acquired on the seat between us in the small cabin of the launch. It was a dark, unfriendly night, and I was steering by compass in the hope of coming out somewhere near the dock on the other side. The chicken kept attacking its image in the window, but other than that it did not seem perturbed by the gyrations of the boat in the stormy water.

Suddenly, just off the starboard bow was a great flurry of lights, obviously a vessel trying to get our attention. It was one of two ninety-foot Abitibi tugboats on Lake Nipigon without so much as a running light to warn of its presence. Mom and I were frightened out of our wits by the near miss.

But that's not all. I wheeled the boat hard over to cross behind the tug, but the waving and the gesticulation and the flashing lights continued with renewed vigor. Suddenly, off to port on the other side appeared a set of navigation lights with two white lights one over the other, signifying it was a tow. Out of the darkness and the spray loomed a huge wanigan (a flat barge with a wooden superstructure). Sick with apprehension, I managed to swerve the launch without swamping just as the tow cable scraped across the deck of our little boat. The wanigan swished through the night close enough to touch it, a white and ghostly face peering at us from a side window, through the spray. As we went on our way I noticed that all the proper navigation and warning lights were now lit for the benefit of whatever other traffic the tug and wanigan might encounter.

Mom and I decided not to make any complaint about the sloppy practice of the Abitibi tug, for we would only bring troubles down on ourselves for being out at night in such dirty weather. We had shaken the feather boa, and were damn lucky to come out of it alive.

During this period of my life I learned that adults are not always the enemies of children, as they are portrayed in so many coming-of-age books. Old men and women are not, because they have time to remember; and maybe ladies when they are in their pie-making mode, and people who are willing to let kids make mistakes and learn from them.

On looking back on it I think I must have been very, very fortunate in the adults I was thrown in with as a child.

From this point on my adventures began to have an adult component to them.

03: How I Found My Vice

Do you remember the beer commercial on TV, the one that ended up with some big, macho hunk saying, "And I knew I'd found my game"? The hunk had a beer in his hand, and a gorgeous "doll" with exquisite boobs by his side, and the ad was supposed to sell whatever brand of beer it was. There were several variations on the ad, but they all showed the hero attending a game, and suddenly getting involved and discovering that the game was the most wonderful pastime since sex. Given the North American propensity to worship athletes and boobs, I suppose the ad sold a lot of beer.

The part of the ad I relate to is the sudden discovery of the wonderful game, only in my case it wasn't a game; it was tobacco. I was about nine at the time I discovered "my vice." The experience had all the intensity of Revealed Truth, and I am sure it was as moving as enlightenment bestowed upon a sinner by a Bible thumper. It was a hell of a lot more real than the athlete with the beer, although I must admit the boobs gave it pretty stiff competition.

Things were tough all over in 1939. My mother and I were visiting her sister and mother in the sleepy little town of DeFuniak Springs in Walton County, Florida. DeFuniak was between Pensacola and Tallahassee, situated in the turpentine woods, and no one had much money. It was a dry county at the time I speak of, although it was my good fortune to be present in the county years later when they finally took the cork out of the bottle.

My Aunt Weedy (really Eloise) worked in a shoe store that catered to country people. Weedy's boss was an open-hearted little guy named Aaron Wohl, who gave away more than half of everything he made. His only pleasure was smoking good cigars, and even this had to be curtailed when things were quiet at the store. Mr. Wohl would cut a number of cigars in two, leaving some in the little apartment he shared with Harold, his young son. The rest he kept in a dish in a room behind the store.

Harold was my age and I used to hang around with him either at the little apartment in the whitewashed frame hotel or in the lane behind the store. For kicks we would steal his father's half-cigars and smoke them in the long grass behind the little hotel. We didn't dare smoke on the street, because everyone in town knew Harold's dad and we would surely have been reported for smoking. Those stolen cigars certainly were good! Smooth!

As inevitably happens to thieves who practice their depredations too close to home, we got caught, probably because one of Mr. Wohl's friends ratted on us. He just walked right up to us and, without raising his voice, he said, "Be at the store when I close it up at six." He didn't even make us put out our smokes.

Harold and I were there at six all right. We didn't think the penalty would be terrible, because Mr. Wohl was a gentle man, but we looked up to him and would never have defied him. Stolen his cigars maybe, but never defied him. We decided to tell the truth when he quizzed us.

"Boys," he said, lighting up another Havana, "I want you to tell me how many of those you have been stealing." We told him it was a couple a day each, maybe more on Saturdays. That sounded like a lot of cigars over a period of time, and we began to have pangs of conscience about the enormity of our misdeeds. We looked at the floor.

My Aunt Weedy came into the room and looked quizzically at Aaron. "Weedy, tell Teddy's mother he won't be home for supper this evening. I'm going to teach the boys not to smoke." He waited until the front door clicked before continuing.

"Now boys, you both know you shouldn't steal. It is wrong. Either you are going to turn out to be thieves or you're not — that is up to you. Right now I am more concerned about the smoking, and I am going to see that you never do it again. Come with me."

Mr. Wohl led us out to the back step and sat us down with a full dish of his half-cigars, perhaps fifteen in all.

"Smoke these, all of them. Smoke these until you are so sick you puke. I will be just inside the back room taking stock. When you have had enough I will take you home." And he left us to strut around the back lane, sticking out our chests and puffing like chimneys.

I thought I had died and gone to heaven. I even ventured to the street at the end of the lane to show passers-by what a great fellow I was. Harold sat listlessly on the step scratching the back of a tired old hound dog that lived in the lane. Mostly he was just letting the cigars burn out by themselves, without puffing or inhaling them. Plainly the exercise was having the effect on him that Mr. Wohl intended.

But not so me. Every puff was a glorious sensation and I even inhaled some of it.

"I knew I had found my vice. I held it to my bosom dearly.
I smoked for over forty years."

Periodically Mr. Wohl would show up and urge Harold to get on with it. He tried to tell us how bad tobacco was for us — mostly that it would stunt our growth. Maybe Harold believed him, but I didn't. Oddly there wasn't a word about cancer or emphysema, the connection with tobacco being only a vague suspicion at the time.

Finally Harold called his dad. "I think I'm going to be sick."

And he was, right out in the lane. Violently sick. At the end he brought up green bile.

"Dad, I promise I'll never smoke again, honest," Harold sobbed as his father led him to the car.

Mr. Wohl told me to keep on smoking — he would be back. When he returned I was leaning on the banker's limousine and practicing flicking the ashes by tapping the cigar just behind the end with my forefinger. Great stuff! I felt like Peter Lorre or Sidney Greenstreet or someone like that, and every puff was marvelous. I understood why bankers and gangsters always smoked cigars in movies. God, it felt good!

It grew dark and the hound dog disappeared. Aaron went back inside, and I continued to be master of the lane. The setting sun glinted off the gold lettering on the window of the newspaper office across the lane. And still I smoked.

Eventually, after a long, long time Mr. Wohl appeared again, asking how I felt. I wasn't feeling all that great, but I certainly wasn't going to let him know it. I pretended I was fine, and to prove it I blew a great puff towards my benefactor. There weren't many half-cigars left in the dish.

"All right, all right. That's enough. If you aren't sick now you'll never be sick. From now on you can take one a day, and go somewhere out of sight of your Aunt Weedy to smoke it! But no more than that, because that would be stealing. And don't tell your mother or your Aunt Weedy what I said."

I was elated. I knew I had found my vice. I held it to my bosom dearly. I smoked for over forty years.

04: A Ride in the Hamilton

I had always wanted a ride in a Hamilton, but in 1942 or '43 airplane rides were hard to come by. Not impossible for a forestry brat, but not something that happened every day. To me, even as an eleven-year-old kid, the Hamilton was a magic carpet. Knowing there were only a couple left in the world, I wanted to be able to say I had flown in one. I collected airplane rides the way other kids collected hockey cards. I waited and bided my time.

The Hamilton was a big, pug-nosed corrugated metal monster that was powered by a 525-hp Hornet radial engine, a great noisy uncowled bug smasher that hung out in front. The fuselage was long and thin, with tail feathers perched way out at the back. Being so far out, the rudder and elevators exerted tremendous leverage, and when taxiing downwind the pilot had to be careful not to let the wind get under the tail, or the machine might just get tossed over onto its back. To make matters worse the floats had droopy noses and tended to submarine in the troughs in anything worse than a moderate sea.

There were no passenger seats or safety belts on the Hamilton, so you flopped among the freight where you could. Usually there were boxes, cans, and folded tarpaulins to sit on. It was not an aircraft for fastidious passengers. I don't think there were any government regulations about seats and belts, but if there were, one simply ignored them.

One day when my dad was away in his leaky old Vedette Flying Boat on an expedition, his pal Winston Buckworth floated down in his Hamilton. In the right hand seat was a young engineer named Hill. They were at Orient Bay to do a couple of trips that my dad would ordinarily have taken had he been home. Buck intended to do what was required, then hightail it back to his own base at Port Arthur.

The chief purpose of the trip was to be the delivery of a grub order to the Deputy Ranger Base at Garden Lake, off to the west of Lake Nipigon. The boys were living on jackfish and bannock, so getting food to them was a matter of some urgency. The Hamilton was to return to Orient Bay for another load to somewhere else before the day was over.

The Hamilton (left) on the ice in Red Lake, Ontario, early 1930s.

Buck went up to the house for a cup of tea, leaving the engineer and me to load and fuel the aircraft. In return for my help in wobbling the fuel up to the wing tanks I was able to enlist the young engineer's collaboration in stowing me away. I made a nest in the grub boxes, and after first exacting a promise that I wouldn't tell Buck he had helped me stow away, he threw a tarp over me. Buck climbed in and fired up without seeing me.

The flight to Garden Lake was uneventful, but I was in real apprehension about what Buck would do to me when I crawled out of my hiding place.

The landing at Garden Lake was hairy. As soon as we lost way and turned downwind the tail started to lift. I could look out through a rivet hole, and I saw the water curling over the starboard float. Buck jammed the column full forward, thus putting the elevators in the down position, which in turn had the effect of blanking off the underside of the horizontal stabilizers and relieving the lifting pressure of the wind. We gradually settled back to the horizontal position, and I breathed again.

I had to show myself at Garden Lake, and Buck was predictably furious, the more so because I had not told my mother I was going on a joyride. He gave me a good, solid kick high up on the butt and said there would be more when I got home. I believed him, too. Trying to hide the tears I climbed back into the airplane to finish the unloading and the return to Orient Bay.

But it was to be several days before we returned to Orient Bay. Waiting at Garden Lake was a message to fly further west to Sioux Lookout, where there was an urgent trip. The flight to Garden Lake was worth a kick in the ass, but I was apprehensive about the tariff for a longer

The Hamilton on floats, like the one in my stowaway trip, early 1940s.

jaunt. I didn't have to hide on this leg of the trip, which was just as well, because by being available I was able to be of real service. That is probably what saved me from serious discipline when I finally got home.

We bored over to Sioux Lookout at all of eighty miles an hour, which was about all that could be squeezed out of the ancient Hamilton with the big Edo floats. Our ground speed against a moderate wind was likely not more than fifty miles an hour.

We touched down into a rolling swell, and as before, Buck turned downwind when the way was off. This was a tricky business, because the ungainly machine wanted to stay weather cocked into the wind. To compensate, Buck gave a little burst of throttle. When we finally came around, we were going pretty fast. Buck momentarily took his eyes off the horizon while he tried to light his pipe. When he let go the control column for just an instant it came back to the elevators-up position with a bang, and the wind immediately got under the tail.

Once more the tail rose and the noses of the floats commenced to bury themselves. The engineer let out a yell and pushed the controls forward. Buck blew out his match and yanked the throttle closed, but the tail hung in the air without dropping back. I felt the hair tickling on the back of my neck as it has done several times in my life when I sensed the grim reaper was making a play for me. I was as frightened as I have ever been, but fortunately not paralyzed.

I made a leap for the rear of the cabin, clambering up the wildly sloping floor, hanging on by my fingernails. I was aware that the propeller tips were digging water and throwing spray back against the fuselage and underside of the big, cantilevered barn-door wing. Buck turned his head and yelled over the noise of the engine, the wind, and the spray, "Go back, Teddy, go back. Go back as far as you can." One doesn't have to be a genius at physics to know that putting weight out at the end of a lever will bring the other end up, so I scrabbled clear back to the rear bulkhead, squeezing into the place where the fuselage narrowed down, hanging on as if my life depended on it, as it very likely did. Looking out I could see the water rudders three feet in the air. It seemed to take forever, but slowly, oh so slowly, the tail settled back down, and I knew I would live to see another day. Buck looked back and smiled at me while he re-lit his pipe, but I noticed this time that he held the column firmly full forward as he did so.

OPAS pilot "Buck" Buckworth, at Orient Bay forestry base, 1944.

At Sioux Lookout the wheels were put in motion to let my mother know where I was and that I was not in any danger. The communication medium could have been Lands and Forests Radio, CNR (Canadian National Railway) telegraph, or perhaps a message relayed over the hand cranked magneto telephones that served the northern part of the province. Whatever it was, I knew that I was not going to be popular at home. For the next few days I stayed in the bunkhouse at Forestry Point in Sioux Lookout and ate my meals in the cookery with the fire fighters. The women in the homes at the base tried to mother me, but I avoided them as much as possible. I guess anyone who was ever a kid will understand why I was on my best behavior.

Several days later we flew back to Orient Bay, pumping the nose compartment of the leaky starboard float before every take-off. When I stepped onto the dock my mother was there to meet me, word of the adventure having preceded me on that network that mothers have. "Been shaking the feather boa, have you?" she said as she gave me a big hug.

05: First Summer Job

In 1943 any self-respecting kid would have had contempt for youngsters with today's work ethic, or lack of it. Some kids are willing to work and learn today, but I am afraid they are in the minority. Today's thirteen- and fourteen-year-olds impress me as shiftless and lacking in ambition — a gormless lot.

It was different when I was growing up during the war, World War II, that is. Perhaps it is not that young people are lazier today, but that the war put pressures on us that just don't exist in this generation. At any rate, most of the boys I knew, and even some of the girls, were anxious to show their brothers and sisters and neighbors who were away at the war that they, too, were worth their salt. Or so it was with country kids. The town kids were not blessed with the same opportunities, but to give them their due, many of them worked in stores or light industry.

At the time I speak of I was definitely a country kid, at least in the summer time. Pop was a forestry pilot and we lived in all sorts of interesting places during the summer, places like Forestry Point in Red Lake, the Shevlin Clark sawmill in Fort Frances, and Orient Bay at the foot of Lake Nipigon. These were my job-seeking, trying-to-grow-up-in-a-hurry years. I was unreasonably jealous every time my older friend and only companion, Eddy Fleming, picked up an honest-to-goodness adult job, leaving me with no one but his kid sister to keep company; hardly an appropriate pastime for a boy who was trying to be a man. Eventually my dad took Kenora as his summer base, but by then I was about fourteen and just beginning to look a little like a man. Jobs were not so hard to come by for older boys, though it was not long until we had to compete for jobs with returning soldiers.

But I am getting ahead of myself.

I was ten the summer of 1942, and I kept after Chief Ranger Doc Gerrard to send me to a fire, or put me on a fire tower, or something. Anything would do, provided it got me away from home. I was too young, of course, and Doc wouldn't do it. The summer came and went and I had only the younger Fleming children to play with, or occasionally the Gerrard children. No job.

The next summer was the same thing. I was allowed to pump gas up into the wing tanks of visiting aircraft, pump the floats, drive the boat to town for the mail, but still no paying job. I really liked the Fleming girls and the Gerrard girls, but I would have died rather than admit it. Don't ask me why. It is the nature of young boys not to admit they like girls.

The next summer was 1944, and I finally landed a job. By now the chief ranger at Orient Bay, adjacent to the village of MacDiarmid, was Whitey MacDonald, who had taken temporary leave of his duties as a sergeant major in the army. When I caught up to him he was bellowing orders to everyone in sight: to fire fighters, the cook, the boatman, and his family. Big, red, and beefy, he inspired terror in me, who was all of twelve years old. I visualized his huge hand with the golden hairs gleaming on the back grabbing me and throwing me like a football into my boat, sending me home humiliated. When I finally screwed up my courage to approach him, the ordeal was not nearly as bad as I had anticipated. I looked up at all nine feet of him and squeaked, "I know about that fire south of Gull Bay and I'd like a job on it, Sir."

I expected Chief MacDonald would take MacDiarmid men and send them to the fire by boat, rather than hiring Gull Bay men. At that time there was a policy within the Ministry to hire fire fighters from a distance, the theory being that people from villages adjacent to a fire might have been tempted to deliberately set the fire in the hope that local people would be hired to fight the fire. In the 1940s men in remote locations had trouble finding work, and they still have to this day. A fire fighting job at four dollars a day and keep was astronomical.

"What the hell do you think you could do on a fire?" the chief ranger growled at me. This was man-to-man talk, and I knew I was getting through to him. I tried desperately not to squeak this time.

"I could hump hose to the fire, I could run the pumps, and I could carry messages from the fire boss to the men in the bush." I didn't want to mention that I could be the cookee (cook's helper). No glamour there. MacDonald abruptly softened up.

"O.K.," he said, "Get on home and get your pack. The boat leaves in half an hour. And, goddammit, be sure to get your father's permission."

I was ecstatic. I jumped into my little forestry branch skiff (it had previously been assigned to me as compensation for odd chores); I fired up the engine and beat it across Pijitawabik Bay to the Provincial Air Base, which was home. I tied the boat up and raced up to the house. It took me all of two minutes to throw a shirt, some underwear, and a couple of pairs

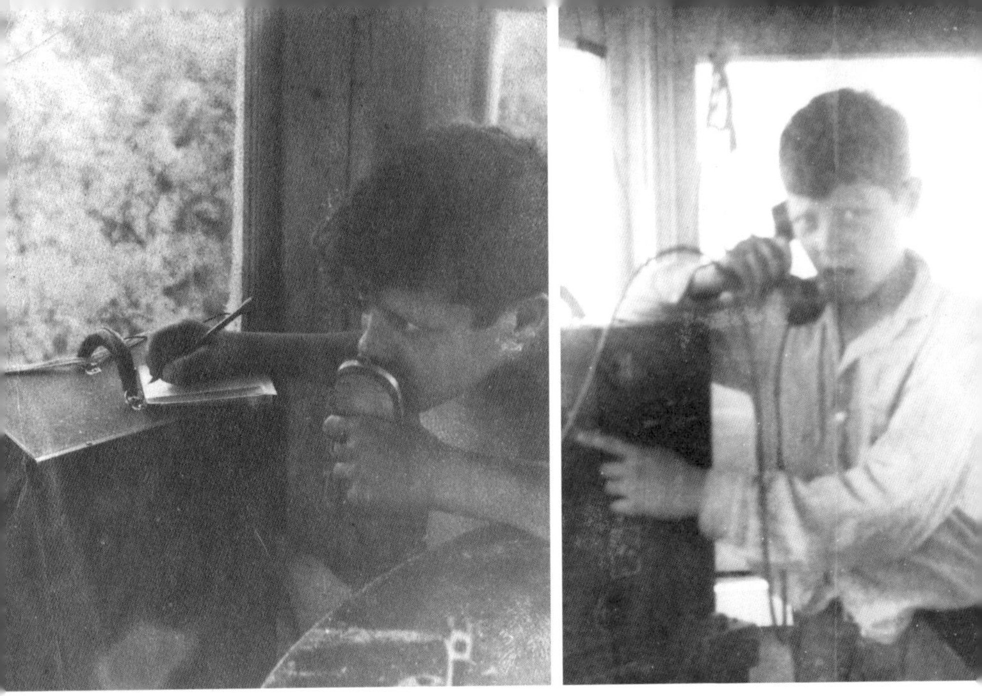

On my summer job, at 13, as tower man, Maria Lake fire tower, 1945.

of socks into a pack. I knew that the MacDiarmid men wouldn't have even that much baggage, that they wouldn't even take their boots off at night.

My parents were highly dubious about the exercise (it certainly was not the last time they were to be dubious about some activity I was about to engage in) but they relented when Whitey Macdonald advised over the hand-cranked telephone that Alex Langilla was to be the fire boss. Alex was well and favorably known to my father as the cook at the Jackfish Island deputy chief ranger station. Pop knew every camp cook within a radius of 100 miles, and I guess he figured Alex would look after me well, even though as a fire boss he was somewhat out of his usual line. I didn't realize it at the time, but Pop was more concerned about the nature of the company I would be keeping than he was about the possibility of my being hurt on the job. A wise man was my dad.

The trip up Lake Nipigon on the forestry boat *Ogemah* (meaning, Boss Man or Chief) was an adventure in itself. Lake Nipigon is full of unmarked shoals, and there were no navigation aids, but the wrinkled old man with the piercing eyes who was the captain was not in the least fazed. I spent the night alternating between a spot on the floor by the engine which was warm, but very noisy, and a place up on the roof of the engine room which was much quieter, but bitterly cold. Just after dawn we came into a rocky pass near Inner

Barn Island, if memory serves, that was completely obscured by fog. The old man closed the door to the engine room and opened all the windows in the wheelhouse. He ordered everyone to put out cigarettes. Poking his nose out the windows, he appeared to sniff his way between the islands; at any rate he said it was what he was doing and everyone seemed to believe him. I think the sniffing was sort of like water witching — there is no real or scientific basis for it, but you can't knock it, because it seems to work. We got through the shoals and tiny islands without touching bottom.

Base camp for the fire crew was to be an abandoned lumber camp on the shore of Lake Nipigon, some five miles south of the village of Gull Bay. This camp featured a couple of habitable buildings and a safe wharf for the *Ogemah*. Alex immediately preempted the more weatherproof of the two buildings, being a corner of the old camp stable, for him and me, letting it be known that we did not want company. The remaining eight or ten men shared the other, more dilapidated shack. There were no beds for anyone. Cooking and eating were under a huge tarpaulin devised by Alex.

Alex would not let me go anywhere near the fire. Not so much as a whiff of smoke was allowed to me. Oh, ignominy! I was assigned the duties of the cookee, and required to wash and dry the never-ending supply of dishes. I heated my water on the portable tin woodstove whenever there was room, and when there was not I washed them in cold, greasy water. Alex had me put aside dishes that had been washed in hot, soapy water for him and me to eat off. Finding wood for the stove was another of my endless chores.

One day while fetching water, which required a careful approach on slippery boom logs, a beautiful, panic-stricken doe ran out onto the logs, no doubt trying to escape the fire. She ran right by me on one log while I teetered on another, parallel to and touching it. The deer ran for several hundred feet on a succession of logs before leaping gracefully into the water and swimming to a nearby point of land. I lost my balance and took a most ungraceful dive into the cold waters of Lake Nipigon. I either leaped to avoid the onrushing beast, or it knocked me into the water as it ran past; either way, I was not covered with glory.

The fire was put out in just four days, no thanks to me. Alex had worked us day and night, but we only got paid the standard four dollars a day, and only for three days. Still, I think we were all satisfied with that. I know that twelve dollars earned money looked pretty good to me, who wasn't even sure that he was going to be paid a dime at the beginning of the exercise. But still, I would have given up the whole twelve dollars just to be able to say that I had humped a bag of hose to the fire.

Summer job at 15: camp cook at a makeshift outdoor cookery at a forestry project north of Dryden, Ontario.

The evening the fire was finally out we all piled into the *Ogemah* and chugged over to the Gull Bay Reserve, where a mammoth party was going on. What the party was in honor of I don't know, but those folks certainly knew how to throw a shindig.

The houses at Gull Bay were all identically fashioned of hand-hewn square timbers, with a plank lean-to off one side. I recall wondering why they were all identical. Many years later I found out. In a close-knit community everyone must behave according to certain norms in order to keep the peace. At Gull Bay one of the norms was that you must not live in a better house or dress better than your neighbor, otherwise it will be said that you are trying to be "higher," thus the identical houses; no one better or "higher" than the others. The sociologists call it the "crabs in the bucket" syndrome because of the tendency of crabs to reach up and claw back into the bucket any crab that is about to escape to freedom. One of these houses had been selected for the party.

Before we left the *Ogemah* at the public dock, Alex had me chain the boat to a timber so that mischief-makers could not cast it adrift. He showed me how to lock the cuddy just ahead of the wheelhouse from the inside, and finally, he covered the forward hatch with hose bags and light equipment so it could not be seen for what it was from the outside. Anyone caught inside simply had to push the overhead hatch cover out of the way, hose bags and all, and scramble out.

I sensed there was tension in the air, but I was too green to ask what all the precautions were for, and of course, I did not want to look stupid. Perhaps the tension was because the local men resented men from MacDiarmid, about 60 miles away, coming in to take fire-fighting money they considered to be their own.

But, now to the party. It roared on in the main room of the square-timbered cabin in which the stove had been removed and the pipes wired up to the ceiling while the participants stood around the walls. The party was fueled by the good nature of the guests, and some really vile home brew. Alex told me I could have one small drink (a "zip" in local parlance) but no more. He needn't have placed the restriction on me because the stuff was so horrible I couldn't bring the dipper closer than six inches to my face.

Music for the party was provided by a three-piece band consisting of a guitar, a violin, and a wicker chair played using a stick and a brush like a whiskbroom, and a whole lot of enthusiasm. That combination actually makes pretty good music as long as one is prepared to listen to something other than the classics. One suspects the enthusiasm component is at least as important as the instruments and the skill of the musicians. A few years later I attended another country-dance at a little place called Localsh up on the main line of the Canadian Pacific Railway where the same instruments were used, but the booze was better, having been purchased from a bootlegger in Missinabie.

The local priest made a tentative appearance to try to lead his flock away from sin, but instead was led to the door himself. An implied threat of violence kept him from returning. At about this time Alex banished me to the lean-to, which I found to be inhabited by an old lady, Mrs. Wigwash, if memory serves, and a number of dogs, each chained to a separate place on the wall. (Mrs. Wigwash was, according to the band records, 117 years old! I learned how old she was because I told my mother about her, and my father flew Mom in to meet the old lady.) The music twanged on.

A while later *Pootawchi* (Round-Like-a-Barrel), the local Hudson Bay Factor, came looking for his children, taking several pretty daughters home with him, but not his son Buck. Buck was supposed to be studying for the priesthood, but his vows were on hold that night.

As the festivities became wilder and noisier Alex was torn between

The *Amik,* a typical forestry boat similar to the *Ogemah.*

inclination and duty, his inclination being to stay and enjoy the party, and his duty being to see that I didn't get into any trouble. Unfortunately for me, duty won out. We spent the rest of the night holed up in the cuddy of the *Ogemah,* sleeping on the life jackets.

On the following morning I awoke to the purr of a Gypsy Moth engine. It was my dad coming to rescue me from the temptations of Gull Bay. On the way home I shared the front cockpit with a Wajax fire pump. These pumps are heavy, hard, and lumpy, and I do not recommend them as seatmates in a single seat cockpit on a bumpy flight. Even so, I had no trouble sleeping.

That was the first and last fire I worked on, and I never got within a mile of it.

Over the years I had many other jobs appropriate to students, and a few that definitely were not. I minded a fire tower on several occasions, I drove trucks, I cooked (in a primitive sort of way) for crews in the bush, I prospected, I worked underground, I ran boats, I railroaded, I worked as an oiler in the rolling mills in the steel plant at The Soo, and more. I even briefly drove a laundry truck for my uncle in North Florida, and even more briefly tried my hand at substitute teaching at Sea Breeze High in Daytona Beach. To be truthful about it, my folks didn't always know where I was or what I was doing. Many of my jobs had to do with boats, and quite often airplanes were in the picture. I am still fond of boats and airplanes. I am moderately fond of money, too, but then as now, enjoying life takes a priority over making money.

It was a darn good way to grow up.

06: The Dirty Old Men of Cameron Falls

My thirteenth summer, or perhaps it was my fourteenth, was not much fun, but it was interesting, if I might make a fine distinction. It would have been more fun if thirteen weren't such a damnably awkward age. I was still a kid, but I was trying to behave like a man and didn't quite know how. The adults with whom I associated must have been hard put to treat me like a human being, to which I am sure I, like most teenagers, had only a superficial resemblance. I had an experience with a homosexual, I met a prostitute, and I had a fight with a grown man. At the risk of disappointing the self-appointed, self-anointed sanitizers of today's bland society, I will say emphatically that these incidents did not scar me for life or victimize me, even for a short period of time. Perhaps they were character-building experiences, but I will let others be the judge of that. Modern-day "victimologists" please take note.

I lived with my parents on a rather isolated forestry air base at the south end of Lake Nipigon on the other side of the bay from the village of MacDiarmid that summer of the last year of the war. Any kid who had the gall to say he could do a man's job was given a crack at it. I could cook for myself, I knew from previous experience how to operate a five-meter radio communications set, and I was at home in boats or in the bush. And so it was that Chief Ranger Whitey MacDonald gave me a job as a tower man at Jesse Lake, a wide spot on the Nipigon River a few miles north of the Cameron Falls hydro project. My mother and father reluctantly let me go.

My partner's name was Tom Aucoin. He was a big, good-natured man who had been invalided out of the merchant marine, having had three ships torpedoed out from under him. Tom was a nervous wreck, and had problems he was reluctant to discuss.

Tom was pathologically afraid of snakes and frogs. I recall an occasion when we were walking down a trail, when Tom let out a yell of terror. Turning, he grabbed my .22 rifle and threw it violently at a crooked stick, thinking it was a snake. I didn't laugh at him, but gave him what comfort I could, and he became my friend forever.

Our grubby little mosquito-infested cabin on the shore of the Nipigon River would normally have been serviced by Forestry Branch aircraft out of MacDiarmid, my dad's base, but one of the last of the great river drives was in progress and most of the time a float-equipped aircraft could not safely land there. Procuring groceries was a matter of hailing an "alligator" that serviced the river drive run between Virgin Falls and Cameron Falls, and heading down through the logs to the Abitibi wood cutting camp near Cameron Falls. For some reason, this always happened on a Thursday. The Abitibi bull cook would assign us bunks in one of the two converted shanty style bunkhouses, and after a silent dinner in the cookery we would make our way to the nearby hydro colony.

The local storekeeper, Mr. Sutherland, would very obligingly open up for us, and we would do our meager shopping for rice, beans and canned vegetables. In that time our four-dollar-a-day wage went a long way in a grocery store, although there were many things we couldn't get because of the war, sugar and butter for example. Meat we had to shoot or catch. The usual pattern was that we would carry our groceries over to the community hall and watch a 16-millimeter movie, then trudge back to the bunkhouse. In the morning we would catch the first northbound alligator back to our little cabin, and one of us would immediately proceed to the tower.

Perhaps I should explain about some of the words I am using before going on.

An "alligator" is a boat with a shield, or cage, around the propeller, enabling it to go through floating logs, provided they are not too tightly packed. Many of them, even the smaller ones, carried large winches capable of pulling boat, passengers, and all over tightly packed booms of logs or even over land for short distances. In an earlier time, steam-driven alligators would even march inland to semi-permanent camp sites towing wanigans — flat barges fixed up with wooden superstructures as sleeping wanigans, cooking wanigans, and horse wanigans — as they went. Such arrangements were no longer in use in 1946, but the smaller alligators survived as a feature of the logging industry until the early 1960s.

A river drive was an organized effort at floating downstream many hundreds, or even thousands, of cords of wood. This wood was cut way back in the bush in the winter and floated down to the mills in the summer, where it was made into lumber or pulp for the paper mills. Wood transportation today is all by truck or rail.

A shanty camp was a long log or framed wood structure that housed a number of men in platforms along the walls. Heat and cooking were by fireplaces at both ends of the building. Most of these camps were replaced, or at least converted to something a little more modern, during the 1930s.Today the bush camps are more like resorts, with proper dining rooms, recreation rooms, and all the amenities.

The bull cook was responsible for getting wood and water to the cookery. He was sort of like a desk clerk or a bouncer in a cheap hotel as he assigned sleeping spaces and looked after the minor problems associated with the camp.

A "cookee" could be a man or a woman. They were kitchen help and doubled as servers at mealtime. Meals were always eaten in strict silence enforced by the cooks. If the men were not allowed to talk they could hardly complain about the food.

On one of these periodic grocery trips, Tom and I were billeted side by side in the less ramshackle of the two bunkhouses at the Abitibi landing. On the other side of me was a rather smelly older man, who only grunted when he was spoken to.

At lights out, I crawled into bed still wearing my pants, as my father had instructed me. My wallet with a few dollars was in my side pocket, and the blanket (there were no sheets) was tucked in under the mattress all around. No one was going to roll me, by golly! There were only a half a dozen men in a camp that would accommodate forty, the rest being out on the river drive.

Uneasiness was upon the camp that night, because of the bears. Most bushmen were very careful about bears, some being almost superstitiously frightened. Contrary to what we learned as children, bears are not furry, cuddly, friendly creatures, but they can be mean and are always unpredictable. They are immensely strong. By the time I was thirteen I had been well indoctrinated with the truth about bears, and the fact is that, like most bushmen, I was scared shitless of meeting one face to face. The camp boss had dynamited a nuisance bear earlier in the evening, out by the garbage dump, and another bear was said to be lurking around the cookery. From time to time we thought we heard it behind the bunkhouse on the trail to the companionable eight-hole toilet, thus creating a problem, which you can imagine for yourself. I drifted off into an unsatisfactory rest, barely under the threshold of sleep.

Much later, I can't say when, I awoke with the feeling that something was wrong. I couldn't be sure, but I thought I heard someone breathing right close to my ear. I lay there listening, eyes still closed. I forced myself to breathe regularly. A movement somewhere on the bed. There! I

One of the bunkhouses at Cameron Falls.

felt it! Unmistakably a hand seeking entry into my pocket, sliding over my hip, and now more to the front. I was actually lying on my wallet, but I had no doubt about what was happening. I was being rolled!

I was lying on my right side, and my assailant was behind me, which meant I had to roll over and strike out with my left hand at an awkward angle in order to defend myself. Nevertheless, I whirled and landed the man a good, solid thump on the mouth that left my hand tingling.

The thief rocked back and said loudly, "What's the matter kid, what are you doing coming over to my bed? You must be having bad dreams."

Immediately the bunkhouse came awake. Men shouted, and someone shone a flashlight my way, clearly picking out the old man from the neighboring bed sitting on the floor next to me, blood flowing from his mouth. I recall being damned angry, but frightened, too.

My partner, Tom, leaped out of his bed and dove over me, fists flailing and knees pumping, landing right on top of the old guy. Within a minute, he was hamburger.

"Stop! Stop!" I yelled. "He didn't get my money. I still have it. It was only a few dollars anyway."

A gruff voice, not Tom's, answered, "Let him be, kid. The dirty old son-of-a-bitch has it coming."

Tom dragged the old man out by the heels and dumped him in the dirt outside the door. He whimpered a little as he bumped down the steps of hand-hewn timber. In the light of the coal oil lantern that had materialized I saw a trail of blood, not just drops but a solid trail that looked black in the flickering light, where the old guy had been dragged.

I sat on the edge of the bed smoking, trying to be like the men. I talked knowledgeably about thievery in the night. One by one the cigarettes ceased to glow, and the men went back to sleep, but I could not.

I waited an eternity for first light, and listened, trying to interpret the noises I heard. That splashing in the washhouse was surely the old man washing his cuts and bruises. There was a rustling and a grunt somewhere that could have been the bears. From my companions there were farts, grunts, snores, and the sound of wet socks dripping on the floor. It was a long, long night. About half an hour after dawn there was the unmistakable clank of the cast iron lid of a wood stove followed by the *shunk-a-shunk-a-shunk* of the grates being shaken. The cookery was coming to life.

I decided to brave the perils of the dirty old man in the washhouse, and the bear out behind, and go to the cookery. I needn't have been afraid. The old man was washing the blood off in the washhouse, and was a menace to no one. The bear, if such there ever was, had departed. It is astonishing how menacing situations are improved by the coming of daylight.

The cookee in this particular camp was a young woman. The camps of that day all adhered to one or the other of two philosophies — either they kept women out of the camp, in which case the men didn't fight, but would leave camp to go to town for feminine company more often; or they allowed women in camp, which tended to keep the men around too, but sometimes they would fight for the attentions of the women and become inefficient at their work. A variation on the second way of doing things, and one which I encountered in later years in camps served by professional caterers, was a system whereby the cookees were alternated between naughty girls who kept the men in camp, and girls with a puritanical streak in their characters — "iron pants" so to speak. Anyway, the Abitibi camp at Cameron Falls sported a girl cookee whose morals may or may not have been better than they should be, but the point is that she was a really good listener. Bartenders and psychiatrists could have taken lessons from her.

As she went about putting on coffee and tea and preparing breakfast I prattled about the bunkhouse incident of a few hours previous. She was very attentive, asking questions now and then to draw me out. As I told it the highlight was, of course, when I socked the old man who was trying to steal my money. She just smiled.

I didn't drink coffee, so she made me drink tea. As an adult I like the stuff, but that was probably the first time I had ever taken a whole mug of it. I drank it because I figured it would make me look like a kid if I turned it down. The cookee sat opposite me with a mug between her hands, speaking earnestly, and told me all about the other half of the facts of life, about homosexual behavior. She spoke in four-letter words, not to shock me (I had never heard a woman use those words before!) but to make sure I understood. With loathing in her voice she told me all about what some men do to each other and to young boys.

What a sap I was! How could I pretend to be a man and not know the filthy, old pervert who took a run at me in the night had no interest in my money, but that it was my warm, pink body he coveted? My ignorance was a setback to my self-esteem.

In the morning Tom and I returned to our cabin on the shore of the Nipigon River. I wanted to talk about what had happened. Tom would only say it was very wrong for men to do those things with boys, that maybe God didn't like it. Other than in our frequent blaspheming, which was more to Tom's French Canadian tastes than mere Anglo scatological oaths, it was probably as near to a discussion on theology as we got all summer. He had no such reticence when discussing women and, after the fashion of lonesome men everywhere, we talked about sex in minute, clinical detail. And like men everywhere, the less actual experience, the more talk. The subject of the cookee and whether she did or didn't, and if she did, exactly what was it she did, kept us busy for a week.

A few weeks later when it was time for a grocery run, Tom decided I should go to Cameron Falls alone. "If you want to be a man you got to act like one. This time, Teddy, you go by yourself. You must learn to do things even if you are afraid." My parents had told me not to short-sell someone just because he didn't have an education, and I recognized what Tom said as the voice of wisdom. When the alligator nosed into shore I climbed aboard without Tom. I particularly enjoyed the six-mile trip downstream to Cameron Falls because it was on a new alligator with a screaming Chrysler engine, and I was allowed to run it, heady stuff for a kid who was trying to be a man.

"Sleep in there," growled the surly bull cook, jerking his thumb at the more decrepit of the two bunkhouses, which was occupied by a few unwashed "fringe specimens." I had heard that bad diseases were prevalent in there, and even without knowing exactly what was meant by the term "bad diseases" I knew damn well I didn't want one. Judging by the state of their unsanitary outhouse, in which the sign that said, "Pee in this Hole" was totally ignored, I could believe it was true about the bad diseases. I had a better reason than that for avoiding it, as I wanted to be in the company of the guy with the flashlight in the other bunkhouse. Tom and the man on the alligator, following the explanation of the cookee, had educated me about some of the less savory practices of lonesome men.

Nevertheless, I knew better than to argue, and I sauntered off towards where I had been directed. When the bull cook wasn't looking I slipped into the other bunkhouse and put my pack down near some younger men who wore clean shirts. Some instinct told me that the company of such people was preferable to the company of derelicts who lacked self-respect. My tongue is not in my cheek when I say this, but I suppose you could put it down to a careful upbringing. I have found this to be a pretty good rule to follow ever since.

The evening and the night passed without incident. I saw nothing of the dirty old man or the bull cook. In the morning I had breakfast and was walking towards the alligator with my groceries when the bull cook hailed me over to where he was sitting in front of the washhouse. He had a large sledgehammer in his hand and was preparing to use it to wedge a log in two pieces.

"Hey, kid, come over here." He sounded angry. I walked over, trying to look nonchalant. "What you doing sleeping in that bunkhouse when I told you to sleep in the other one?" The bull cook was furious, and as he rose to his feet I could see his hand was shaking. As he spoke, a hand-rolled cigarette bobbed in the middle of his dark red face, and he waved the sledgehammer at me.

I figured I was in plenty of trouble, and I didn't want to give him either of my real reasons for avoiding the older bunkhouse. There were several men standing around, but I did not know if I could rely on them to help me in a pinch. I gave the man a weak little smile that was intended to be placating and said timidly, "I don't like the shithouse that belongs to the older bunkhouse." It wasn't my real reason, but it was the truth.

I didn't intend it to be funny, but God knows I was scared out of my wits. A burst of laughter came from the bystanders, prompting the bull cook to snatch the cigarette from his mouth and glare at the ring of men now pressing in. I figured some of them might be on my side. The red-faced man redirected his attention to me, stepping forward, the sledgehammer still in his hand. As he did so he put the cigarette back in his mouth, burning end first. He let out a yell that made me shiver, and silenced the onlookers. "Aaah", he screamed as he pulled the cigarette away, leaving little red flecks of Vogue cigarette paper on his lip. "Aaah, you little asshole."

It is difficult to remember with accuracy every little detail after more than half a century, but I have a picture of the man's face turning from dark red to purple, his eyeballs protruding from his head. In his upraised arm was the sledgehammer. I only had a split second to think, and it would only be guessing if I told you what raced through my mind, but I can tell you I was damn scared of that sledgehammer.

I stepped towards the bull cook and kicked him with all my strength right in the jewels. My caulked boot sank into his groin with about the same effect his sledgehammer would have had on my skull. He fell to the ground like a rock, gasping. His face was filled with a gratifying amount of surprise, pain and confusion, but at the same time I noted an alarming amount of hate. I don't spend a lot of time in examining the morality of my past because the result of too much introspection can be madness, but I have to confess that to this day I wonder if he really deserved such a draconian kick in the balls. Maybe he was only fooling, which would have made the punishment inflicted on him excessive indeed. So, years later I have to say that I just might have overreacted. But then, maybe not…

One of the spectators helped me gather my groceries, giving some sound advice as he did so. "Young fella, I'd get on that alligator and get the hell out of here fast, and I wouldn't come back this way if I were you."

I didn't need any urging. Having seen the action with the bull cook, the boatman had thoughtfully put the alligator in gear. This time it was an ancient alligator with an old three-lung Russell engine for power. I was comforted by its steady *pung…pung…pung…pause…pung…pung…pung* as we made our way upstream, but I wished it were faster. I kept looking back to see if the new, faster alligator might be coming along with the bull cook aboard.

My father must have heard about the incident with the bull cook at Cameron Falls through his grapevine. A few days later, in the early morning during a lull in the log drive when the river was clear, he landed his big yellow Norseman in front of our cabin and taxied in to shore. As I took the rope and snubbed the aircraft to a tree he shouted, "Get your pack together. We want you at home." He didn't sound pleased.

I was sorry to say goodbye to Tom Aucoin, but I knew my dad was right. It was time to go. I wasn't a man yet. Maybe I could have another shot at being a man next summer.

While on the subject of dirty old men, I want to say that they seem to thrive in small, isolated communities. In another, totally unrelated incident, I organized a geology field trip to Wawa while I was a student at Michigan College of Mining and Technology, Soo Branch. One early summer evening a group of us students was walking down the main street, trying not to kick up dust, when we noticed a couple of unsavory looking gents sitting on a bench outside a local store, their attention obviously on two young girls in summer shorts who were out for a stroll. A lot of winking and nudging was going on between the old guys on the bench.

One of the two gents made a comment in an unnecessarily loud voice about what he would like to do to the little girls. The children were horrified and veered towards us for protection. They walked with us for a block or so until they could take refuge in a familiar store, leaving the dirty old men snickering on the bench.

A few days later, back at college, we had an assessment of the trip, what we had learned in the field, and what the experience had meant to us.

One well-bred young lad from Detroit piped up and said he had learned a great deal of technical value from the field trip, but he had decided he would be leaving the course at the end of the term.

"What made the biggest impression on me was the realization that I would be spending a good part of my life in little mining towns. No doubt I will marry and have children like those two little girls we saw on the street in Wawa. I simply can't stand the thought that dirty old bastards are going to be hanging around making suggestive remarks at them, or worse. It's not normal, and I'm not going to allow it to happen to my children." We didn't scoff or snigger.

I was devastated that this event was the culmination of the expedition I had so painstakingly organized. Our professor, Ernie Kemp, put it in perspective for me when he commented, "Better he find it out now than after he finishes his geology course and actually takes his family to some little mining town off in the boonies."

07: Surgery in the Bunkhouse

We were a pretty congenial bunch of guys in the bunkhouse at Ball Lake in 1948. The boss, Barney Lamm, was a good man to work for, and he provided us with a warm, dry place to sleep and three square meals a day. On top of that, he paid us ten dollars a day plus whatever we made in tips from the high-rolling tourists we catered to at the fishing camp. But there was no such thing as sick leave or a medical insurance scheme.

You know how it is, as you get older. You tend to forget names. Fifty years later I still know people who were at Ball Lake that magic summer, and I have had to talk to some of them to refresh my memory as to names. There was Ed, Bill, Peter, Larry, two Richards, Henry, Einar, Ivan, and a whole raft of others. In particular, there was Big John, Old John, and Young John. Big John happened to be old and Young John happened to be big, which complicated matters when you had to refer to one of them. There was also Keith Roseborough who, at seventy-five, was the oldest man in the camp, and he also took credit for being the wisest. Keith lived to be over 100, and till the day he died he liked to tell about the time he took the boil off Old John's ass. Or was it Big John's ass? I know it wasn't Young John's ass because it was too wrinkly to belong to a young man. I have forgotten, but it doesn't really matter.

Old John was one of the more successful guides in camp. His guests never got skunked, and his tips were huge. One day he got seventy-five dollars for two days' fishing, an astronomical sum. He had some beer and wieners flown in, probably at the boss's expense, and threw a Saturday night beach party for the staff. We knew that seventy-five dollars wouldn't pay for all that beer, but Old John said it was okay because he would make the balance in tips the following week. We ate, drank and were merry, and many were the toasts to good old, Old John.

Within a couple of days we realized that John was in some sort of physical difficulty. He stood to eat his meals, and padded the seat of his boat, an unheard-of luxury for a mere guide in those days. He became cranky, too, but no one wanted to take issue with him because of his recent generosity at the beach party. Behind his back we speculated unkindly about a variety of loathsome diseases, many of them social in nature, which might be causing John's problems. In a glorious moment of self-pity, John finally told us, his mates in the guides' bunkhouse, that he had a boil on his butt, right at the point that took the pressure when he sat down. We all found this screamingly funny, and I must admit that I laughed as hard as anyone else. For years I thought it was really amusing, until one day I developed a boil in a rude place myself. After that I was sorry I had ever laughed at poor John. I suppose my boil was divine retribution for my amusement at his plight. When that happened I thought back to that wild morning at the guides' bunkhouse at Ball Lake...

Barney didn't want the sufferer to leave camp, for he would miss at least a day's work if he went into town, more if he stayed there and went on a toot. The camp was full of guests and Barney needed every guide he could get. John didn't want to leave either, as he couldn't afford to miss the pay and the tips. Besides, he just didn't want to pay a doctor's bill. But he was in agony and wouldn't have been of much use in his condition even if he had stayed.

Keith Roseborough saved the day for John and his boil. Well, almost. Keith had been a bushman all his life, and had mushed dog teams for both the RCMP and the Hudson's Bay Company before the turn of the century. He had been married to Native women on several occasions, after the custom of the country, and had absorbed bush lore about the cure for various ailments. Keith said he would be happy to take the boil off, but he would need four people to help him. We soon found out why he needed the four helpers. He should have asked for six.

The plan was for John to lie down on his stomach and expose his afflicted butt to Keith's ministrations. Keith was to place a pre-heated wide-mouthed bottle over the boil and create a vacuum by pouring cold water over the bottle, sucking the boil out, leaving a neat round hole, which would not infect but would heal over painlessly. That was the plan. Sounds simple, doesn't it?

Peter, who wanted to become a doctor, was allowed to help in the process. It was an honor. The other young people, including me, were not. Only older, steady men were delegated to hold John down. The rest of us had to be content with being spectators.

Nor was it to be a co-ed exercise. Trixie, a tall, blonde, beautiful Swede who was one of the cabin girls, produced clean towels, hoping this act of mercy would earn her a place as a spectator, but she was banished in spite of her good intentions. Florence, the other cabin girl, was young and gorgeous but, with her parents employed at the camp, had no hope of getting anywhere near the guides' bunkhouse.

Gurgling on the old wood stove in the centre of the room was a pot of water with a beer bottle, a quart milk bottle, and a ketchup bottle, all clean and sterilized.

Keith had John lie face down on a bunk near a window, where the light was good.

The self-appointed medical personnel peeled off John's trousers and opened the flap on his long johns (he wore them all summer — never took them off as far as anyone knew), and were presented with a huge, horrid, putrescent, quivering, yellow protrusion surrounded by multi-hued aureoles.

Keith positioned the bottles over the boil one at a time, like a gentleman trying on bowler hats for size at a haberdasher. We watched closely, totally absorbed. First, Peter handed him the beer bottle. Keith shook his head. John groaned. Dead silence in the room. Twenty spectators held their breath, not knowing what was coming next. The bottle was too small.

Peter then selected the milk bottle for a trial fit. Keith held it up, turned it over and made a great show of lowering it to a position just over the boil. John's fundament quivered in anticipation as if he had eyes in the back of his…well, never mind. The bottle was too big. I thought of Goldilocks sitting in the chairs.

As he took the bottle away, Keith inadvertently let a drop of hot water fall near the boil. John jerked and screamed, "Yeesus Christ, what the hell are you trying to do, kill me?" The four men who were pinioning his arms and legs knew they were going to have a real job to do.

Peter grasped the wide-mouthed ketchup bottle between two sticks and Keith took it in a clean towel. We all strained forward. It was juuuust right, a perfect fit!

A bottle of whiskey materialized, courtesy of Barney. Keith took the bottle of whiskey and poured some of it over the boil. He refused a drink himself, as he figured it would be contrary to the Doctor's Oath for the surgeon to have a drink, or something like that. Peter, who was fifteen, had no such scruples and downed three fingers of it before holding it up to John's mouth. John swigged at it until he gagged. Many years later when Peter actually was a doctor he admitted that it was only by a magnificent effort of will that he kept the whiskey down, as he didn't dare disgrace himself before his peers. In later life Peter never again suffered from this disability.

The moment arrived for the big operation. Keith called out, "Hold him tight, men," and eight hundred pounds of brawn clenched their jaws and immobilized the patient. "Yeesus Christ, Yeesus Christ," he hollered over and over.

Keith plopped the hot bottle down firmly over the boil while Peter poured cold water over it. The effect was as planned. It cooled the bottle down fast and created a vacuum that drew the contents of the boil into the bottle. John screamed bloody murder, and one of the men holding a leg grunted, "Hurry up, will you, I can't hold him much longer." By this time, John's breath was coming in short gasps and he was straining like a bull elephant in a trap.

All eyes were on the bottle, which was bobbing and waving about like a stubby glass tail. Closer watchers noted a great bulge of proud flesh creeping up into the mouth of the bottle. All of a sudden, the boil broke with an audible pop, spattering the inside of the glass with blood and pus. The viewers all recoiled in disgust, and the man holding one of the patient's legs involuntarily relaxed his grip.

The fateful instant was all John needed. He kicked out and knocked his keepers away from his legs one at a time. The stalwarts holding his arms did not loosen their grip, but John was strong enough to rise from his bed of pain, screeching in agony, carrying them along with him. The obscene glass tail came along behind. We spectators cleared a wide path.

"Yeesus Christ, take it off, take it off!" implored John.

"Hold still, you dumb Swede," yelled Keith, as he made a grab for the bottle. He gave a mighty pull, but only succeeded in fastening it on the tighter. By this time, you could see where John's bottom was being sucked way up into the bottle, no doubt causing serious injury to the flesh. John and his tormentors lurched into the stove, knocking it to one side, allowing the stovepipes to fall to the floor. Soot scattered everywhere, and the room began to fill with smoke. Water sloshed from the bottle sterilizer directly onto the top of the stove, creating steam, which further obscured the vision. Over the din and confusion, John's voice could be heard, now an octave higher, bellowing "Yeesus Christ, yust break the bottle, qvick before it kills me!"

Someone took a swing at the bottle with the back of a blade of a hunting knife. The glass was too tough. Keith made a grab for the knife and swung the knob on the handle at the bottle. Glass and blood went flying everywhere, and Keith's fingers were cut where he had gripped the knife blade while swinging it. John's bum exhibited a neat round hole the size of a .45 slug surrounded by a fiery red patch of flesh the size of a small plate. With every heartbeat the hole jetted out a stream of blood. He was in a semi-fainting condition and flopped on his belly on the nearest bunk. Keith calmly poured more whiskey on John's poor, battered bottom, and this time he didn't hesitate to have a little snort himself. Then he poured some on his cut fingers. In a burst of masochism Peter downed the rest.

Barney came in and looked sadly around at the devastation. He didn't have to tell us to clean it up. He just shook his head and walked out.

Old John had to be flown out to Kenora after all, kneeling on the floor of the Parson's Airways' Foxmoth, swaddled in bloody towels like a gory New Year's baby. Keith went with him to get his cut fingers looked after. Keith was back the same day, but they kept John in the hospital for most of a week. Barney let him rig his fishing boat up with a special padded chair for the rest of the season.

I have always wanted to do the boil-in-the-bottle thing to someone myself, purely as a scientific exercise you understand, but to this day I have never encountered anyone else with a boil who would consent to undergoing the procedure.

Perhaps I can get a job in a tourist camp again. It would be a shame for the world to lose such precious knowledge.

08: Shenanigans at Goudreau

When I knew Goudreau in 1950 or so it was a little village of fifty people, very much in decline from its former population of 3000. It had a peak during World War I when it thrived on the mining of siderite and pyrite, two ores that were valuable for their iron and sulphur. The village went into decline when a better means of extracting sulphur was developed in Louisiana and one-half of the reason for its existence disappeared. During the 1930s there was resurgence in the fortunes of the community when the market was right for gold, and a half-dozen small gold prospects within ten miles became profitable. Rising costs and highgrading by employees were responsible for decreasing profits, and the last of the little gold mines that supported the town closed in the early '40s. The closing wasn't dramatic. People just walked away from their shacks and homes, in some cases leaving the remains of their last meals on the tables and clothes in the closets. They took the train to other little communities along the Algoma Central Railway (ACR), where a living, of sorts, could be gleaned, or to the southern terminus of the railway at Sault Ste Marie, which represented civilization in that part of the country and still does in the early 21st century.

The people trickled away, all but a handful not dependent on the mines for their livelihood. Many of the buildings simply fell down and there were a few destructive fires. What was left in 1950 was a ghost town, populated by people who were waiting for something better to come along, and by souls that haunted the abandoned buildings. What came along was Algoma Steel's subsidiary, Algoma Ore Properties, the mineral exploration company for which I happily worked. The local people's hopes for a better world to come caused the residents to treat the exploration crews very well.

When I got off the train in the early summer of 1950 I found my crew of fellow prospectors boarding with the Cappalini family, one of the two large Italian families in the village. Mrs. Cappalini was a member of the local three-person Board of School Trustees. She was unfortunately not on good terms with Mr. Deconto, the head of the other large Italian family in Goudreau, also a member of the school board. Wilf Gagne, an older member of my crew who had his home in Goudreau, was the third member of the Board.

The School Board had never functioned very well because of language problems and a certain lack of good will on the part of the Italian two-thirds of its members. Wilf Gagne usually signed for everything the schoolteacher put in front of him, including dutifully concocted minutes of meetings which were never actually held, thereby satisfying some far-off bureaucrat in Toronto that all was well in Goudreau. No one could recall the last time a school inspector had appeared in the village. At about the time of my arrival the schoolteacher was involved in a dreadful car accident, and had to leave. As far as I know he never returned. This left the three trustees without a secretary, as in that antediluvian time the teacher was also the secretary to the Board in remote areas.

I think the real reason the school continued to run satisfactorily was that there was oodles of money available to pay the way. The Algoma Central Railway had freight yards and freight sheds and paid taxes on it all. Algoma Ore Properties and several other outfits had iron ore claims within the township, and the tax money rolled in, enough to keep up the two room school with its little library, pay a teacher more than she deserved, buy enough stove coal for the school and every residence in the town, and pay a mentally disabled man to push it around in a wheelbarrow, with some left over. All this for just six children between six and fourteen years old!

At some time during the summer the School Board ceased to function at all, and I was pressed into service as an imported person — one who theoretically was not engaged in school board sniping — to be a runner between Wilf Gagne and Mrs. Cappalini and Mr. Deconto. In effect I became the executive officer and general secretary to the Board. There was no election, no appointment, it was just something that needed doing, and so I did it.

We embarked on a hunt for a teacher. It wasn't easy, in spite of all the money there was for extras, as Goudreau was out at the edge of the earth, accessible only by a 170-mile day coach ride from The Soo. There was a road but it only went seventeen miles over to Localsh on the CPR and only in dry weather. Localsh was equally isolated, and in every bit as serious decline as Goudreau.

Labor Day was just around the corner when we finally hired Priscilla from Niceville. We had to promise her $2,800 a year and extra time off, when the going rate was $2,200 for a girl just out of teacher's school.

Priscilla turned out to be a hell of a good sport considering she was a

Home base during exploration jobs for Algoma Ore Properties, 1952.

protected little flower from a small town down east. We taught her to cuss, shoot partridge, and drink beer, all necessary skills for survival in Goudreau. She held school whenever she could corral more than four pupils at a time, and the children loved her. On rainy days my partner Tony and I would visit with her class and tell them tall tales. The fragmented school board seemed to be happy with the situation as Priscilla wasn't sleeping around, and she was available to teach four days out of five.

I left Goudreau late in the fall, some time after freeze-up. I worked for a while in the Helen Mine at Wawa, which was also an enterprise of Algoma Ore Properties. I drove a laundry truck in North Florida, for my uncle, and I worked for a few months as an oiler in the rail mill at the steel plant in The Soo. I may even have re-entered the dunghill of education for a year, but perhaps not. There has been a lot of water over the dam since those days and I simply cannot recall the sequence of what I did from month to month. But one thing sticks in my mind, and it is that I eventually worked for Algoma Ore Properties again, and returned to Goudreau.

Goudreau was much the same as it had been when I left a year or so before. But Priscilla was gone by now, and in her place was a Mrs. Calverly, who was demanding an audit of the books, which were not quite in order when Priscilla left. I was vaguely acquainted with Mrs. Calverly's husband, who had been banished to the Wawa–Goudreau area by the exploration division of Jones and Loughlin Steel in the States. He was an accountant who lived at an abandoned mine near Wawa, simply known as The Josephine. Most weekends he could be found in Goudreau with his wife. In his spare time, when not managing Jones and Loughlin Explorations, he prospected on his own behalf in the Goudreau area, and consequently fell into the same relationship with the School Board that I had had the previous year. Now it devolved on Calverly and myself to audit the School Board books.

The audit took only one evening and was simplicity itself even for a mathematical illiterate like me. It took place on a plank table covered by a gray blanket in one of the few habitable rooms left at The Josephine. Income was determined from bank statements, expenditures by a few cancelled checks and a handful of chits and receipts. It was all there in a shoebox, plain to see.

And what we saw was that Priscilla had not accounted for $700, quite a sum in that day. I was disappointed that Priscilla would make off with money that was not hers, but not concerned for the school board coffers, which overflowed. I suppose we wrote to someone in the Department of Education in

Toronto, but we took no active steps to recover the money. After all, hadn't we told Priscilla to be sure to spend all that tax money? Besides, we liked her, and that made the duty of ratting on her quite distasteful.

I corresponded with my parents quite frequently, telling them about the people I met and the places I went. I must have told them about Priscilla's defalcations. One day in a letter from my dad, he mentioned that he had met Priscilla, now the wife of a free trader near an Indian reserve somewhere in the North. I tapped into some long forgotten reservoir of righteousness and determined to get that $700 back for dear old Goudreau.

It was easier than I thought.

I wrote Priscilla a letter, not an accusatory letter, but a friendly one, more or less, congratulated her on her marriage and her new baby and told her about the people back in Goudreau. I mentioned in passing that Calverly and I had had some trouble with the audit, and we couldn't account for $700, and could she help me?

She could, and she did. Back came a cheque for seven hundred and some dollars, and a perfectly logical explanation (remember, this was 1951 or 1952, and things were not as they are today) to the effect that at the end of the school year Priscilla had $700 left over. She didn't want to simply leave it in the shoebox in the teacher's desk in the school, and she thought it would be impolitic to leave it with either of the warring school board trustees. Wilf Gagne was out of town when she left, so the only thing to do was to take it with her. She intended to get it back to Goudreau somehow but forgot it in her effects back in her parents' home in Niceville when she decided to get married. Her stuff was eventually put in storage, and her life became distanced from the purse with the $700 in the storage box. Her pangs of conscience were not great, as she knew there was lots of money to keep the school afloat back in Goudreau. Nevertheless, it was a tremendous relief to be presented with an opportunity to put the money back where it belonged, without recriminations. Years later, after I had undergone the metamorphosis from average citizen to Crown attorney, I wondered how I would have reacted to Priscilla's story if faced with it as an explanation for the wrongful possession of stolen goods, or with theft. I probably wouldn't believe it today…but half a century ago? She could have been telling the truth.

Mike Porobich was another one of the Goudreau characters. His wife and daughter, Dolly, ran a little country store that looked like a remnant from the turn of the century, which it was. You could actually buy a large, functioning carbide lamp from him for fifteen dollars, or a knitted cardigan sweater jacket for three dollars. When not busy working at the Helen Mine in Wawa, Mike often lived in a shack a few miles out of Goudreau, rather than at the store. No one knew why. Mike walked with a waddle that made one think he had a porcupine up his ass, and indeed he had one of the world's worst cases of piles.

Mike had been told he would have to go down to The Soo, and perhaps all the way to Toronto for a hemorrhoidectomy, and he dreaded it. He decided he was going to do it himself, and to facilitate the operation he purchased several bottles of whiskey, a fresh pack of Gillette razor blades and a small mirror.

On a long weekend when he was back from the mine Mike ensconced himself in his shack in the bush, which was situated a few yards off the road to Localsh. I wasn't in town at the time, but I got the story when I returned and I believe it too, because Mike still walked like a bull with a porcupine in a rude place. Anyway, Mike proceeded to get roaring drunk, and with the aid of the mirror he tried to cut his piles out. He succeeded in losing a terrific quantity of blood, hurting himself badly, and scaring the living hell out of himself.

Fortunately for Mike, an old lady lived near enough to hear him yelling when she left her house to visit the little shack out back. She went to his door and poked her head in and saw what was going on. With great presence of mind she stuffed a shirt up Mike's bum, gave him another drink, took one herself, and ran into the village to sound the alarm.

Mike was not particularly well loved by his neighbors, but they nevertheless rallied around to save his life, which was fast soaking into the mattress. One of the few vehicles that would still run was brought to the door and they loaded him in the back, face down. Mike was humiliated beyond words, with his poor abused bottom hoisted in the air for all to see, a bloody shirt hanging out like a soggy, red flag. He must have felt like he was in a tumbril being paraded to the guillotine.

The whole village was present to boost Mike up to the caboose of the next southbound freight train. The ACR was always good about stopping in emergencies, and the conductor quite willingly agreed to take Mike to the Red Cross station in Hawk Junction, where they stemmed the crimson tide.

No one ever dared to mention the matter to Mike, but I guess he never did get his piles properly fixed up because forever after he walked in a funny way.

Mike Porobich wasn't the only one in town with a self-destructive bent. There was Enos McAskill, a sometime diamond driller. Diamond drilling is a really tough, dirty job and it has been my observation that only men with a very high tolerance for pain, discomfort, and grease can stand it for long. Enos McAskill was such a man. In fact he tolerated these adversities so well that his neighbors wondered if perhaps his mind or his sensibilities were not working very well. You will too, when I tell you what happened.

Prospecting for Algoma Ore Properties, Goudreau area, north of Sault Ste. Marie, Ontario.

Once in a while Enos's carnal desires proved too difficult to control, and it was his habit to relieve the pressure by visiting a rather low-down and dirty establishment in Hawk Junction that accommodated sportin' girls who weren't too particular about whether their customers were clean. As a matter of fact the girls themselves weren't too clean, and the preferred object of Enos' affections was no exception. One day a couple of weeks after a visit to Hawk Junction Enos noticed that all was not well in the plumbing department. Something green was issuing forth.

A member of his family, who was smarter than Enos, figured out what had happened, and persuaded Enos to go down to The Soo, to the health unit. As expected, they diagnosed a case of the clap. Penicillin was new and the clap bugs had not developed a resistance to it, so it was not long before Enos was on his way back to the drilling camp, apparently cured.

A few weeks later Enos again felt the urge and he paid another visit to his ladylove in Hawk Junction. It is not really part of the narrative, but I have to speculate that the health unit had not yet been able to search out the offending young lady in order to neutralize the bad bug she was handing out to her johns. At any rate Enos, in a display of monumental bad judgment, went back to the same girl in the same house and got the clap again, presumably in the same way he got it the first time.

This time it was bad, real bad. It happens that disease-causing germs often become immune to medication that is repeatedly applied to them. Such was the case with the germs in Enos' system. They had become used to penicillin, and simply laughed off efforts to destroy them with the same stuff. It took repeated injections of different strains of penicillin before something worked to restore Enos' plumbing to order.

What happened to the girl at Hawk is not known to me. Nor do I know if Enos ever smartened up, as I have not been back to Goudreau since those two summers more than half a century ago.

Algoma Ore Properties maintained two main base camps in the Wawa area. Besides the Goudreau set-up, in which we either rented an apartment from the Cappalini family, or boarded with them, we had a camp at the Firesand River, just a couple of miles off the dirt road that ran between Wawa and Hawk Junction. There were other semi-permanent camps, but for the most part we set up fly-camps if our work places were more than a few miles from the base camp.

The camp at Manitouik Lake was one of these fly-camps that were an outpost of Goudreau. *Manitouik* means a spirit with evil connotations, but does not translate well. Being well aware that it was a dangerous lake, as the wave action could be sudden and treacherous, we had a healthy respect for it, and didn't venture out if there was a wind during daylight hours. You could paddle in to it from several directions, or you could fly in, but you always had to be careful.

A rather strange sequence of events occurred while we were at Manitouik. One day all the boys but me got laid low by summer flu, and lounged around in their tents feeling sorry for themselves. We had lots of Spam and canned soup, and enough ingredients to make bread, but not much else. A passing flotilla of boys from an upscale summer camp in New York State made inroads into our Spam and soup, leaving in the middle of the night while there was no wind, expecting to be at the far end of the lake by early morning. I was really the only able-bodied person in camp so, Fred Rivers, the cook, volunteered to supervise while I made bread. Making himself comfortable in a nest in the contours of the woodpile, he directed me in the mixing, kneading, and rising of the dough. It took several hours, and the sun was coming up when I popped three bread pans into the oven of our portable wood stove. Marvelous! Fresh bread to go with that damned Spam and soup!

But it was not to be. Something went wrong, and all three loaves deflated in the oven. What should have been three delicious football sized loaves came out as three hard lumps the size of large baseballs, totally inedible. We made the mistake of eating it anyway, fresh out of the oven. We ran out into the rain and wind to retch on the ground, away from the tents. I said it was just the flu, but the boys preferred to believe it was the bread.

Things were mighty gloomy at the Manitouik fly-camp the next morning. We couldn't go to work because the wind prevented us from traveling on the lake to our work sites, and we didn't feel like it anyway. We made solitary resting places in the tents or close to the stove under the huge tarp that sheltered the crude split pole table. Occasionally someone would go out to tighten a rope against the rising wind. We contemplated our misery, wondering when Holly, the company pilot, would be dropping in with a grub order.

That was the way matters stood when two strangers walked up to the camp from the shore. They were forestry employees on some mission, traveling in a smallish canoe with an outrigger on a rack on one side and a two-and-a-half horsepower kicker on the other side near the stern. It looked like a bastardized rig to me, and it was certainly grossly overloaded, and quite unsafe. The men stopped long enough for a cup of tea, but politely decided to go on their way when they discovered we were low on grub. We begged them to stay, citing the anger of the spirit that ruled the lake and our own experience of it, but no, they were certified foresters, and they knew better. After a second cup of tea they puttered off directly into the frothy waves. Verdun Venn, who was our party chief at the moment, shook his head and made a gloomy prediction.

We returned to the contemplation of our navels in the various hidey-holes we had constructed for ourselves. The wind shook the tents, and we would shrink away from the bursts of rain that found their way in through the cracks.

An hour after our visitors had left we heard a noise at the shore and looked up. Standing by the half-filled canoe was one of our forestry visitors, stark naked except for a hernia belt, leaning on a pulp stick. There was no sign of his partner or of their effects. Trouble! We ran to him and half carried him to a place by the stove. Fred produced a hot drink, and Wilf rubbed him down with a towel. Someone loaned him a pair of pants and someone else a shirt. We wrapped him in a blanket and pushed him nearer to the stove. After fifteen minutes of our ministrations he was able to gasp out his story.

He told us that immediately upon leaving our camp they began to make heavy weather of it. There was some protection from a point of land a few hundred yards farther on, and they decided to see how it was beyond the point. It was a mistake of considerably greater magnitude than merely eating hot unrisen bread, and it was fatal to one of the two canoeists.

About one hundred feet around the point their misbegotten outfit surmounted a wave and nose-dived into the next trough, taking on so much water that it could not climb over the next wave crest. They had no time to bail or throw out gear as the canoe wallowed in the trough. The next wave simply overwhelmed them, and they found the canoe sinking under them, stern first. They probably had no life jackets, as such frippery simply wasn't used in those days; in any event, they weren't wearing any.

Both men struck out for shore, which was only fifty feet away. The survivor who lived to tell the tale was nearly a non-swimmer, and he hung on to a floating pack. The other fellow was supposed to be a good swimmer, but he disappeared within the first three or four strokes. The survivor hung on to the floating pack, and after a terrible struggle managed to reach shore. The bow of the canoe was just above the water and he followed it down wind parallel to the shore until the stern grounded. Eventually he managed to catch a dangling end of twine with a stick and pull the canoe to shore. He had no memory of removing his clothes (we later found them on the shore well away from the water) or how he steered the half-full canoe back to our camp. Fortunately, it was directly down wind.

We cranked up our little portable high frequency radio set, one of the first of its kind, and by some miracle got it to work. Some quirk of atmospheric fate prevented us from reaching the office in The Soo, but we were able to talk to a bush camp in Quebec. They in turn contacted their principals in Montreal, who contacted our Sault Ste Marie head office with the tale of woe about the missing forester, who we presumed was drowned. By mid-afternoon the wind began to drop and we were able to commence dragging operations.

Dragging isn't really the word for it. Manitouik Lake was a hydro reservoir lake. The tree line had been cut back, and the wood salvaged. When the lake rose, it covered stumps to a depth of fifteen feet near the shoreline, very effectively preventing a dragging operation. Bobbing with a treble hook and a weight was the best we could manage. We didn't snag the body but we retrieved several packs of gear and a can of watery gas for the little Johnson kicker.

Speaking of which, thank goodness it was a Johnson. With the aid of a pair of pliers and a bent nail sharpened like a screwdriver blade we were able to dry the motor out and get it going. We decanted the gas into a glass jar and poured off the water, and were in business. We couldn't have done it with any of the other popular makes of the time.

For supper we had Spam and Campbell's soup and tea — nothing else. God, I learned to hate Spam by the time the expedition was over! After dinner Verdun and I patrolled the shoreline with the outrigger contraption, concluding that it was a death trap even without a load.

Manitouik Lake was a different place the following day. Planes flitted in and out like dragonflies, one of them even bringing in a load of fresh grub and some cigarette tobacco. A policeman showed up, the Forestry paid a visit, and a relative of the deceased thoughtfully brought in some whiskey. Dragging (or bobbing) began in earnest.

This was a bad day for me. My mates were pretty well recovered from the flu, but I was coming down with it; nevertheless I was expected to be active. It damn near killed me.

Fortunately it was all over by mid-afternoon, when someone snagged the dear departed by the ear and brought him to the surface.

A cedar strip boat came in from the far end of the lake and served as a temporary coffin. Dragging it up broadside to the shore, the policeman reverently placed a blanket over the body. Trouble was, a hand was sticking out just as if it were trying to clutch at a clump of grass at the shoreline. The deceased's brother leaned down and piously took the hand, shoving it down inside, tucking the blanket in firmly. A sigh of satisfaction was heard from the onlookers.

But the body was not amenable. The blanket stirred and the hand slowly inched its way out again, impelled by rigor mortis. There was much clucking of tongues by those watching, and surreptitious signs of the cross by the Catholics.

The policeman, feeling compelled to master the situation, murmured a respectful, "Allow me," and leaned down by the gunwale. He took the errant hand and quite forcefully shoved it down beside the body, rolling an oar onto the hand for good measure. He tucked the blanket in again, and stood up. The brother, influenced as much by whiskey as by emotion, dabbed at his eyes and stood at the very edge of the bank. A sigh of approval drifted up from the crowd. We thought the policeman had done a really fine job.

A close watcher might have seen a preliminary stirring of the blanket, which would have given warning, but I don't think there were any close watchers. I, for one, was expecting the bank to collapse, thereby pitching the brother into the boat with the departed. I watched him in secret hope.

Quite suddenly the blanket flew up, the oar flipped out, and the dear departed's hand flew out and actually slapped his brother on the foot. The brother stepped back and sat down with a yell of consternation. This was not as satisfactory as if the brother had actually fallen into the boat on top of the dear departed, but it was thoroughly gratifying nevertheless. The crowd groaned, either in disapproval or an effort to stifle amusement.

I returned to my tent to sleep off the flu, trying not to throw up. It is an odd sensation to hold in laughter till one's belly hurts and to want to upchuck at the same time.

After a day or so all the people went away and we had to get back to work. Work consisted of studying the details of an airborne magnetometer survey that pinpointed magnetic anomalies, comparing the survey to stereoscopic photographs, then going to the spot on the ground and locating the actual anomaly, and checking it out. Sometimes we would do two or three a day if they were close. At other times it might take several days just to locate a single anomaly, and check it out with a dip needle. The work was really quite congenial, if one could ignore the heat, the mosquitoes and the black flies. The companionship was of the first order, and the food was excellent when not restricted to Spam and canned soup. Did I mention how much I came to detest Spam?

I was still ill with the flu when we started on a two-day side trip to an interesting anomaly. We paddled, four of us and gear, for an hour, hid the canoe, and walked inland for several miles. It was a dreadful trip. My pals had to carry my share of the gear as well as their own, but they were good natured about it. I tagged along with only my own little pack. The bugs were voracious, it was all uphill, and we disagreed on the best route. Dinner that night was a tight-lipped affair, until it was time for dessert.

About the only thing I contributed to the exercise was chocolate. I had taken along a part tin of powdered cocoa, filled to the top with sugar and powdered milk. The lid came off and the stuff was all mixed up in the bottom of the pack with underwear (clean), sticks and debris. We were so desperate for energy food that we used it anyway. I shook my pack out into a pot of water and heated the whole mess up. The sticks and debris were so thick we had to strain the sludge through a clean handkerchief. The gooey stuff wouldn't flow, so my mate Tony took a jackknife and stabbed holes in the handkerchief. He caught the resulting goo, which seemed to be as much leaves and debris as cocoa, and we watched with anticipation as he took a long sip. "Aaah," he said, "It's perfect. It must have been that last twig that done it!" We all roared with laughter and held out our own cups.

With that we forgot our grievances and became pals again.

Next day we found our anomaly. It was a banded iron formation all right. It gave a few strong readings, but was so localized as to be uninteresting. The iron band was only a few inches wide, but what we'd hoped for would have been several feet or more across. For some reason it showed up as huge on the magnetometer graph. All that work was for nothing.

That remote location just a few miles north of Lake Superior was the sort of place one could look at and say, "Surely I am the first human being to have ever set foot here!" But in fact we found blaze lines that looked to be forty years old crossing the anomaly. That meant some prospector in about 1910 had been poking through the bush and stumbled on it quite by accident. Bear in mind they didn't have magnetometers, airplanes, or even accurate maps in those days, just dip needles. I have a lot of respect for the ancient prospector who won his way through that dense bush on a purely speculative trip. Later, in discussing it with my dad, he told me he had been in even more remote places in the Yukon and the Northwest Territories, and had never failed to find a tin can, a piece of wire, or something to indicate that he was not the first.

When we arrived back at our fly-camp on Manitouik Lake we were two days behind schedule, partly because of the flu that we all had, and because of the drowning. Important work was waiting for us elsewhere, so we decided to travel back to Goudreau at night by the light of the moon. By that time I was feeling quite fit, and to make up for my lack of contribution to the tough trip of the two previous days I elected to paddle. Several of the boys came with me in the big canoe, burrowing into the gear and making themselves comfortable. The others had preceded us with the small canoe on the company plane.

A heavily loaded canoe is not hard to move in dead calm water, and with my conscience as motivation I was able to make most of the way without assistance.

Some time just before first light, when the moon was still high, the route took us across a beaver pond. It was coolish, with tendrils of fog weaving eerily through the overhanging trees and hanging like Spanish moss. I considered waking the sleepers up to appreciate the beautiful sight, and was about to do so when there was a great swirl of water just off the bow of the canoe.

A moose! A bull moose with lily pads hanging off his rack, so close I could hear him breathing. Frankly it scared hell out of me, as with two great lunges he would have had us all in the water, no doubt with disastrous consequences.

The big fellow was silhouetted in the moonlight quite plainly but I doubted if he could see our canoe. Drifting slowly, I sculled with the paddle ever so silently, without raising it out of the water or touching the side of the canoe. As we ghosted by I could have reached out and touched his nose with the tip of the paddle. He was sniffing the air, sensing he had company, and backed up uneasily till he was on firmer ground.

A little while later when the boys woke up I told them about the moose, but they said I was BS-ing them. I was furious until Wilf admitted that he had been awake and had held his breath along with me as we passed the unfriendly fellow. Truth is I have always been afraid of moose, having had several adventures with them over the years. Bull moose are not supposed to be dangerous except in the rutting season, but I don't believe it.

Wild critters were always interesting to me, but never a passion. I never thought of becoming a naturalist, but as a kid I read a lot about animals and their habits. I read all the boys' books by Ernest Thomson Seton and similar authors, and books on woodcraft and survival in the wild. They made it sound so easy: boy goes into forest primeval with nothing but jackknife and emerges at end of summer fat and happy — that sort of thing. One of the few places in all of Ontario where that would still have been possible in 1950 was the Goudreau area, which was loaded with every kind of wild animal imaginable, including animals that were not thought to be compatible in the same area, such as wolves and lynx, deer and moose. Partridge and rabbits were so numerous we wondered what they found to eat. As a matter of routine we knocked off partridge with sticks or axes. Now, at the beginning of the new century, I doubt if there is anywhere left where game is so plentiful.

Every morning when in residence at Goudreau, we drove some distance out the single-lane dirt road of which the other terminus, seventeen miles away, was Localsh, up on the main line of the CPR, east of Franz. Like clockwork we would encounter a grizzled old moose in nearly the same place. The old guy would wait till we were about 100 feet away and then he would turn and run ahead of us down the road, which was like a corridor, with high underbrush growing right up to the edge on either side. One day we clocked him at thirty-five miles an hour, but we prudently dropped back when clods from his feet were thrown back and through the open front window. He would have creamed us! When he got to a suitable turnout he would let us go by, peering over the top of the wall of brush with his cloudy eyes. At the risk of succumbing to anthropomorphism, I say that the moose was amused rather than annoyed by these encounters. As you may have guessed, I never turned into a mighty hunter, and I blush to say it in this macho age, but I never have shot a moose. If I were hungry enough I would do it, but not otherwise.

But getting back to Moosic, as we called him. One morning we chugged by him as usual, in our tired old jeep with the plywood cab. As usual we had our little race and went on our way. On our way home in the afternoon we passed by a huge brick stack, which was a feature of a long-abandoned mine. There, fifteen or twenty feet up the iron ladder was Wilf's little daughter Yvonne and her friend Brenda Cappalini, hanging on and yelling at the top of their voices. They wouldn't come down till we drove the jeep right up to the bottom of the stack.

We put their two bikes up on top of the jeep and sandwiched the kids in the cab with us. Between shivers and sobs we got their story.

After school on that beautiful fall day the girls rode out on the road. When they got to Moosic's usual resting place he was not there, so they decided to ride on, chatting as they went. They heard a noise behind them and looking back, saw Moosic, right on their tail! They were quite justifiably terrified, and made speed to the safety of the stack.

Some of the boys made light of the predicament of the two little girls, but I wasn't sure. It wasn't even fall, the season when moose often become combative. I think the girls had darned good reason to climb the stack. Of course the children did not need to be told to avoid the company of bull moose after that.

For a little backwater of fifty souls, Goudreau had a whole lot going on.

There was the incident of the itinerant preacher who stayed with a family while the man of the household was away on a job. He got off a freight train in the middle of the night and, upon finding the preacher in his house, assumed the worst. He beat hell out of the preacher, sending him sprinting into the bush, and as a final touch burned all the preacher's clothes. I was there the next afternoon when a policeman came in on a freight train to resolve the situation. The preacher came running out of the bush, sans pants, and put himself under the protection of the policeman, the much-venerated Constable Waito from Wawa, who was the only policeman in the whole area. We thought Constable Waito would arrest the man who beat up the parson and burned his clothes, but instead he arrested the parson.

It seems that the parson was a phony who was going up and down the line, holding services in the villages, and collecting big donations. Constable Waito had been looking for him. I didn't think what he was doing was all that bad, provided people got their money's worth of hell-fire and damnation, but someone had complained. Constable Waito asked around for a donation of a pair of trousers for the parson, and that was the last we saw of him.

Then there was the time the whole village came down with measles, all except one old lady and myself. The lady, Mrs. Nelson, made soup by the bucket and twice a day I hauled it around on a child's wagon, a five gallon pail of it, doling it out to whoever thought they could hold it down.

And there was Dolly Porobich, who kept store and drove her father's two-ton 1935 International truck about like a madwoman, terrorizing the village. Dolly was "sixthteen" and talked with a "lithp" and had big "breathts" and every male between sixteen and sixty was in love with her.

After fifty years I remember all these things, and more, some of which had best never be exposed to the light of day. When I am old and the end is in sight I want to go back to Goudreau to satisfy my curiosity about what happened to it and its inhabitants.

The years I spent growing up in the bush were good years, and I enjoyed every minute of them. These years helped me finance my higher education and were building blocks for what was to come.

09: Animals

I have always been uneasy around wild animals, and the larger the animal the more uneasy I was. Over the years I had quite a few encounters with wild animals, such as bear and moose, but I did them very little harm except once in a while when I was hungry. Actually, I expended considerable effort in hiding my fear of wild animals from my mates, feeling that it was not manly to show fear of wild critters. Later in life I learned that most sensible people are pretty cautious about getting on the wrong side of wild animals. For years I was only comfortable alone in the bush when I had a .30-06 in my hands. Those never seemed to be occasions when I ran into an angry bear or a succulent moose.

Let me tell you about one of those occasions. It was at Algoma Ore Properties' Firesand Camp, and the year was about 1951.

It was a hot day in mid-summer. All the boys had gone to town, but for some reason I did not, preferring to remain at camp with Fred Hooper, our octogenarian cook, who was full of interesting stories. About mid-afternoon Fred decided to take a nap, leaving me with no company and nothing to do. I decided to investigate the mineralization in a hill a couple of miles away that could be seen from our camp. To get to the hill I had to walk around the hard rim of a pothole lake in the middle of a swamp. I had with me only a knapsack containing a compass and a few sandwiches, and a prospector's axe, which is simply a light axe head hung on a comparatively long handle.

I got to the hill without any difficulty. It didn't take long to discover that there was no visible mineralization of interest in the locality. I sat down on a comfortable log and rolled a smoke, contemplating my next move. As I sat there I thought I could hear noise coming from the direction of the little pothole lake. Following an old game trail, I crept quietly, quietly back to the pothole.

I was half way around the edge when there was a sudden explosion of pond lily roots and a mean-looking bull moose appeared (as far as I was concerned they were all mean looking then and still are), his rack fes-

Algoma Ore Properties staff at Firesand Camp, 1951. Wilf Gagne (center), Fred Hooper, cook (left).

tooned with vegetation, peering at me myopically through his garland of weeds. The old gentleman sensed my presence and immediately declared war. He managed to gain hard ground just as I drew abreast of the only sizeable tree on the edge of the pond. I dropped my shoulder pack and the little axe, scrambling up the tree like an overgrown squirrel.

No one could ever tell me why that old moose was so hard to get along with in mid-summer. According to the hero stories the old guy should have been docile as a lamb in mid-summer, but that was far, far from the truth. He let me know that he was going to mop the ground with me, and he would have too, if he had caught me. Every time he returned to his dinner of pond lily root I would slide down the tree, snatch my pack and axe, and run a little farther. Glancing back over my shoulder I would see him coming, and I would hastily climb the nearest sizeable tree. Eventually, after three or four trees, I put enough distance between us to cause the moose to lose interest in me. I trotted wearily into camp.

I wanted to take the camp rifle to deal with the moose, but Fred Hooper wisely talked me out of it, saying, "Teddy, that old fellow probably weighs over 1500 pounds. How in hell would you get it back to camp on a hot day like this? And who do you think would butcher it? Not you, and for damn sure not me! And how would we keep it without ice?"

Reluctantly, I allowed myself to be persuaded. I chalked up another one for the feather boa. We didn't get any meat out of it, but I got a hero story that was good for re-telling many times. In the beer parlor in town it was good for two, or even three, beers on a hot summer day.

A few weeks later the boss dispatched me to town to pick up the camp jeep, which the Jones and Laughlin boys had stolen early in the summer. Jones and Laughlin was a large steel company in the US and their local contingent of young prospectors had thoughtlessly left their jeep in plain open sight for us to borrow early in the season, and they were now retaliating by holding our jeep for ransom. It was fortunate that we did not take these depredations too seriously, as later on that summer the J and L gang stood up for me on the train when several slanderous men unjustly accused me of taking their beer.

It was a cold, miserable day, and I hoped to catch a ride when I reached the main road that ran between Hawk Junction and Wawa. I kept looking over my shoulder, hoping to see some traffic.

At last, through the mist and the rain, there loomed a vehicle. I kept looking back, willing it to stop for me. Suddenly it was right there behind me, and it wasn't a vehicle at all! It was a curious cow moose. I stepped out quicker, and so did my new girlfriend. When I slowed down she slowed down too, but not very much. The net effect was that she drew closer and closer. I had no idea if she was hostile, perhaps protecting a nearby calf, or if she thought I was a calf in need of protection, or if she was just plain curious. Before long the lady was literally breathing down my neck, causing me to decide to break the impasse. I had been well indoctrinated by old-timers about the damage a moose could do with its heavy fore feet, and I wanted no part of it.

Quickly removing my plastic rain jacket, I turned and whirled it right in her face, toreador style. I may have even yelled, "Beat it!" But if I did it came out as a squeak, because I was just too darn scared to make hero noises. At any rate the lady got the message and she eventually eased off into the bush.

I was vastly relieved when a woodcutter in a beat up old half-ton finally stopped for me.

Contact with bears is much more common. I have found myself in close proximity to many bears, but they are quite unpredictable, and are mean and dangerous. In spite of hearing numerous stories about how someone made friends with a bear, I have always avoided them.

Erica has had several face-to-face encounters with bears, both at our summer place on Cloverleaf Island on Lake of the Woods, and here at our home on the outskirts of Thunder Bay, but has been fortunate not to antagonize them. At one time we caught several in live traps for later release by the Ministry of Natural Resources in remote places. We are believers in the proposition that bears are bigger and stronger than human beings and should be left alone. The bears, also, prefer to avoid contact with humans, and given half a chance and not cornered, will usually put distance between themselves and humans. The exception is a mother bear with cubs, whose instinct is to protect her young ones by showing aggression.

When I was a kid (see the story about the Dirty Old Men of Cameron Falls) I saw the dynamiting of a bear at a lumber camp north of Nipigon, and it was not a pretty sight. That particular bear had persistently raided the camp's food supply for several days and was not amenable to being driven off by less persuasive means. A few years later I helped an old man fashion a spike collar to trap a bear. Between these two incidents I had enough of killing and blood to last me for life. Other than a couple of deer that have been unlucky enough to cross my path, I have only shot small game. As a matter of fact I believe firmly, if not fanatically, that there ought to be room for nature's critters to live on this earth unmolested by people. If you wonder why I disavow fanaticism, it is because I like to eat these same critters, and it would be hypocritical to make a lot of noise about killing them.

So, if anyone wishes to drop off a nice trout, or a juicy roast of moose, you can be assured that it will not go to waste.

10: MedEvac By Night

Sending us off to the bush to hide from Sir James Dunn was probably the smart thing to do. Hell, it was the only thing to do. The alternative was to leave us in the Windsor Hotel, and it was a sure bet that Sir James would be living there for some part of his visit to The Soo, because he had just bought the place. It was said he had bought it for the specific purpose of firing a chambermaid who had the temerity to vacuum his suite after being told not to while he was still in residence on a previous visit. At least that was what we believed. It didn't make any difference that she was right off the boat and couldn't understand. That was probably one of those factoids, or urban legends, that one hears from time to time, but we believed it implicitly, and so did everybody in The Soo.

We were a rowdy bunch of non-conformists and our bosses figured, probably correctly, that we might do something to annoy Sir James, as we considered the Windsor our home. We — meaning Algoma Steel's exploration crew, the shining knights — were mightily p-o'd about the chambermaid. Oh yes, and did I forget to tell you that Sir James Dunn was the major shareholder and chairman of the board of Algoma Steel? He was our boss, about ten levels up. He flew about in a Grumman Mallard with scented water in the toilet while we, his minions, were relegated to bush planes such as the Norseman and the Beaver, both on floats.

The place they sent us was an abandoned mine site some thirty miles north of Sault Ste Marie, as the crow flies. The only feasible way in or out was by air, so we were sure to be there as long as the company wanted us to stay. Holly, the company pilot, said he would bring us some grub in a week or so if old Sir James were still in town. We all felt a little twinge of abandonment as the big Norseman taxied out to the middle of the lake and took off towards The Soo.

We hadn't much to do other than make a pretense of poking around the bush looking for mineralization. The area had been thoroughly prospected back around the time of the World War I, and we knew we would find nothing. Wilf Gagne, a professional bushwhacker, was middle aged, and the only man in the crew over twenty-five. The party chief, Roy James, was a university man, but he very sensibly deferred to Wilf in all matters not related to the location and identification of banded iron formation, of which we knew there was none. When Wilf decreed that we should concentrate our efforts on sleeping and fishing, Roy did not object. The only one who really had to work was Fred Rivers, the cook. The others on the crew included Verdun Venn, Mel Eamon, Tony Paradis and me.

Somewhere on the property we found two ancient cedar strip canoes with hogged backs from which the canvas was falling in large, irregular flaps. Wilf produced a large needle while Tony and the rest of us gathered spruce and balsam gum, which we melted down and used to seal the seams, just like the voyageurs of old. *Voila!* Two rickety, but serviceable, canoes. Actually, you don't need to go to great pains to seal a canoe this way, as water pressure alone will almost do the job of holding a loose flap of canvas against the side of a canoe.

Several old boards were whittled into paddles, not the kind you'd find in a sporting goods store, but pretty darned good all the same. I roughed them out with an axe, and Tony finished them by using his axe as a scraper. Tony was so good with an axe that he could actually shave with it. We had a lot of fun for a few days, but as I recall it we didn't get many fish. It was too early in the season for swimming.

Mel's trouble began on a Sunday morning. He woke up feeling tough, saying he had a bellyache and wanted to lie low for the day. That set the tone for the rest of us. It was blustery and rainy and rather than go exploring a nearby abandoned mine as we had planned, we decided to follow the pattern we had established of reading and sleeping. Occasionally Mel would take a little walk out to where we had nailed a log between two trees to make it easier to obey a serious call of nature. On one of these trips he was overheard to groan. Worrisome.

Mel's bellyache became serious in the late afternoon. We knew he was in real difficulty when he couldn't keep his tea down, but lay all doubled up on the pine bough bed in his tent, which he shared with Wilf. None of us had first aid training, but we understood enough to know that it was probably acute appendicitis because his belly was tender low and to the right. We stood around looking sorrowful and nudging him with our toes and asking if it hurt. It did! After the tenth or twentieth such ministration he asked us not to do it any more, and Wilf shooed us out of the tent.

Roy James called a council of war. The wind had blown the lake to a white froth, and we felt it was unsafe to use the canoes, but it nevertheless seemed to be the only thing to do. We all volunteered to be paddlers, and Fred wanted to go too, but Roy wanted him to stay behind to keep a light on and hot food in the oven. Fred said later that waiting alone, not knowing if the rest of us were alive or dead, made it the longest night of his life.

We hoped that the wind would drop in the evening, as it often does in that part of the country, but there was no such luck. We assumed the risk and decided to leave just before full dark.

We knew that the Algoma Central Railway, which runs from Sault Ste Marie north to Hearst, passed by our lake somewhere near the far end, perhaps a mile through the bush. Tony and I left about an hour ahead of the others, using the smaller canoe. As the heavyweight I took the stern and Tony took the bow. Usually the better paddler takes the stern, but there was a leak of frightening size near the bow and Tony wanted to be where he could deal with it if it got out of hand. We paddled like crazy men, screaming at the waves to keep our courage up. Lightning flashes showed us the way, and also scared the bejesus out of us. I tell you, there was certainly no shortage of adrenaline in our blood! It was the wildest ride of my life, and more than half a century later I remember it as if it was yesterday.

Fortunately, the wind was at our backs and we made good time. Even so, Tony had to flop backwards off his butter box seat several times to bail his end of the canoe and try to stuff rags in the leaks. We contemplated the rearing and plunging with terror in our hearts, wondering how the other canoe with the patient lying in it would bear up under the punishment, not knowing where it was, or even if it had left yet.

We struck it lucky at the far end, as the lightning flashes showed us the way up a creek that took us within a few yards of the tracks.

The year was 1950 or 1951, and railways still had work gangs stationed every five or six miles at section houses. We knew that if we could get to a working telephone we could have a southbound freight train stop to pick Mel up to take him to The Soo in the morning, or have the railway officials send a speeder out to pick him up. All the section houses had telephones.

I set off at a stumbling run hoping to find a section house near at hand. Tony set off in the opposite direction. There can be absolutely nothing more tiring, or harder on the toes, than running on railway ties in the dark. It seemed to be all of fifteen miles to the section house, but in reality it was probably not much more than five. I would have passed it by in the utter darkness if it were not for the kerosene storm lantern someone had left right in the middle of the tracks. The storm was at its height, and with it the lightning, the only friendly thing in the whole universe being that wonderful winking yellow light. I knew it must have been left there for a purpose, and some instinct that I cannot logically explain told me it might even be for me. Upon peering about I could sense the loom of the track gang tool shed, and behind it the austere frame house where the section foreman lived with his family. An orange glow from a coal oil lamp at a side window told me someone was up. It was about three o'clock when I knocked at the door.

To my complete amazement the foreman's wife was awake and expecting me. She even had hot tea and apple pie all ready and waiting.

The explanation was that when Tony and I split he only went a few hundred yards before he came on a section house and equipment depot. He raised the alarm and they managed to raise a railway signalman in Sault Ste Marie, who in turn patched them into the regular phone lines, and thence to an ambulance service. It was Mel's good fortune that there was a bush road from a distant highway to the trackside equipment depot, and the ambulance drivers were familiar with it. Without any assistance from me, an ambulance had been dispatched an hour before I had reached my section house.

While waiting for the ambulance and while I was still stumbling in the opposite direction, Tony and two of the section hands drove a speeder back down the track to the creek. The storm was still raging, though not with its former intensity, and the night was at its blackest, but the paddlers in the big canoe saw the headlight from the gas car shining out over the swamp grass and were able to find their way up the creek to the landing. Mel was lying in the water in the bottom of the canoe, more dead than alive. It had been a hell of a trip, just as bad as Tony's and mine, and they had had to take Mel out of his sleeping bag in case the old canoe broke up in the waves.

They stretched Mel out full length on the section gang's gas car and ran him back to the bunkhouse to await the ambulance.

It must have been at about the time of the arrival of the ambulance that I walked into the section house several miles further north. In the meantime the two foremen's wives had been on the old-fashioned hand crank phones that connected the section houses to each other and Sault Ste Marie, comparing notes. Tony's section lady had waited until the lightning abated, then phoned ahead to tell the lady in the next section house to expect me. That is how it was that tea and pie were waiting for me.

They managed to get Mel to the hospital, but only just barely in time. Somewhere en route in the canoe, on the gas car, or in the ambulance his appendix burst, but the doctors were able to open him up and mop him out, saving his life. He credited his toughness to the fact that he was from the Ottawa Valley, and therefore not to be put down by a mere burst appendix. As tough as he was, it took him many weeks to recover.

After doing justice to the section lady's pie and tea I walked back to the creek, but more slowly this time in order to preserve my toes from the ties. It was breaking dawn by the time I came upon Tony, crouched under a piece of canvas, swatting flies while waiting patiently by the creek.

In the aftermath of the storm the trip back to camp might actually have been pleasant had we not started out cold and wet. It was full daylight when we stepped ashore to a pot of Fred's tea and a mountain of flapjacks and bacon.

The sun was shining brightly. It promised to be a beautiful day.

11: The Man From Heartbreak Ridge

Further in my quest for adulthood is the incident of the returned soldier who panhandled his way across the State of Michigan. I am sorry to say I rode on his coat tails. He pretended to have been in association with American soldiers who had been killed or wounded at Heartbreak Ridge, a notorious battleground in the Korean War during the 1950s. Even today, in the New Millennium, remembering Heartbreak Ridge causes the patriotic American eye to go misty, for a lot of good red American blood was spilled in that battle.

It was the spring of 1954. My friend Pat Newman and I were all through with university. We were leaving the University of Western Ontario, also known as the dunghill of education, as my mother used to say. Pat's wife, Marie, had preceded him back to Western Canada, while Pat and I were towing their house trailer back west with a rickety '30s vintage van that was seriously worn out and fit only for the junk yard. We had no food and only a few dollars when we left London, Ontario but, after the fashion of young men everywhere, we were full of optimism. Something would turn up, we firmly believed. And turn up it did, in the form of the spiffiest looking Canadian soldier to ever stick his thumb in the air.

From the passenger side of the vehicle ahead of us emerged a khaki-clad figure that oozed confidence. From the shine on his shoes to the knife-edged crease in his trousers, and from the knot in his tie to the lines in his face, you just knew: THERE IS A MAN! Pat and I were both impressed by the fact that he went to stand directly under the sign that said "No Hitch Hiking" on the Customs and Immigration building at Port Huron, on the American side of the international border. We looked at each other and one of us said, "Let's pick him up," so we did. He was utterly plausible, and I would probably be damn fool enough to pick him up again today, although Pat claims he would not. Perhaps Pat has made it through to adulthood and his judgment is better than mine, although I am still working on it. As I write this we are both seventy years old.

We thought we had really hit the jackpot with our new rider. He paid for gas, meals, cigarettes, and chocolate bars, enabling us to progress in fits and starts across the State of Michigan (there was no highway around the North Shore of Lake Superior at the time), if not to live well. We were grateful for his presence for a while, and we even let him sit in the front passenger's seat while either Pat or I crouched in the back of the van with the assortment of baggage and tools. We never actually saw him pass money at a cash register, but somehow we were always waved on our way by the proprietors of the seedy joints we usually stopped at.

As we lurched along, the soldier harangued us with tales of his deeds and misdeeds as a member of a Canadian unit attached to the US forces in Korea. We believed him, because we didn't think he would have the nerve to wear a Canadian uniform with a chest full of ribbons unless it was true. Eventually he confided that he had been cashiered without ever setting foot outside the States and Canada or ever pulling a trigger. They (whoever that was) fired him out of the services and took his uniform away. He acquired another one, probably by theft, and lit out for Western Canada. He claimed he was dismissed for some piddling, inconsequential reason. Eventually Pat and I realized that the soldier's largesse at the beaneries was due to theft and fraud when one of us heard him lying to the old lady at a cash register. We agreed that we had to get rid of him, but he had been good to us and we didn't know quite how to do it without a scene. We each had about three dollars in our pockets, but the little fridge back in the trailer contained a few bottles of beer and wine, a loaf of bread and some deli stuff, courtesy of the soldier, and several cans of gas rattled around in the back of the van. We dithered and decided to drive on.

The opportunity to get rid of the soldier fell into our laps like a platter of gold.

We decided to spend our last few bucks in an outwardly seedy Mom and Pop restaurant in Superior, Wisconsin, which you pass through just before Duluth, Minnesota. There was a satin Purple Heart in the window, a sign that someone in the family had been wounded in the service of their country.

During the meal the soldier suddenly stood up and went to the cashier, a sweet little old lady. Some instinct made me sneak up behind the soldier and surreptitiously listen to his conversation. It went something like this: "I was with your boys at Heartbreak Ridge. One of 'em carried me down on his back, and he got decorated for it. I got this here wound stripe…etc., etc." It must have sounded good, for both of them let tears fall to the counter. *Plink, plink!* Between tears, the old lady said they had lost their son in Korea, and she would not take our money. I figured that if I were honest and created a scene the old lady and half the customers would create a riot and maybe beat hell out of us.

We kicked the soldier out within a block. It was not even on a corner, just on a crummy street in front of a bar that didn't have a Purple Heart in the window. He thought we were crazy, but we weren't crazy enough to give him back his food and beer. Because of the nagging of our very impractical consciences we returned to the old lady and tried to pay her with our few remaining shekels. The family poured out of the kitchen, and instead of berating us they plied us with a pie and other goodies to help us on our way. We didn't mind the soldier stealing gas and food for us, but the bit about Heartbreak Ridge was just too much to swallow. Later we saw the soldier whizzing by in a big truck, flashing us a big grin and a "V" sign. Who said that crime doesn't pay?

We laid over for a day to earn a few bucks pumping gas and raking leaves, or anything to make a dollar. Pat worked through the day and into the night. I went to bed early, with the understanding that when I woke I would commence to drive, leaving Pat to sleep in the trailer. This was strictly illegal, but when you're twenty-one who the hell cares.

Our old Dodge panel truck was getting wearier and wearier by the yard on Duluth's hills, and climbing the steep grade was just too much for it. The clutch began to burn. Knowing I was about to lose the clutch altogether, and in the certain knowledge that the rusty mechanical brakes would not hold if the rig ever stopped moving forward, I elected to take the next right turn which would, in theory, take me down the side of the hill and to safety.

But safety there was none. The street turned out to be a dirty back lane with unpainted fences, abandoned vehicles, and garbage lining the sides and filling the ditches. To make things worse the lane was a dead end. Worse yet, I got hopelessly mired in mud and the rain was coming down in buckets. I gave up and went to bed back in the trailer, full of apprehension about what Pat might say in the morning.

Daylight had not yet arrived when I became aware that my nose was hurting dreadfully. Someone was trying to wake me up. The reason for the pain in my nose was pressure from a large caliber revolver that was being pressed against it by an irate father, who was convinced that we were secreting his daughter in the trailer. I still quiver with indignation when I think of the nasty things the man thought we were doing with his daughter.

Pat, the world's champion sleeper, was absolutely no help. The men of "Piggy Lane" concentrated on me, being the only one who would respond. It gradually dawned on them that there was no girl in the trailer, nor had there been one. With that the situation became reversed, and with the exception of one or two who would have liked to beat the snot out of us just on general principles, the locals were full of apologies, and bottles of beer, and sandwiches. A tractor and a truck materialized to pull us back to the street and on up to the highway beyond the hills of Duluth.

It had been an extraordinary day and night. I learned for the umpteenth time that poor folks are really quite generous in comparison to rich folks. This does not mean that I wouldn't rather be rich than poor. As a matter of fact I am a firm believer that it is better to be rich and unhappy than poor and unhappy, but when you are on your uppers I say go to a poor man for help every time.

Pat continued to sleep in the trailer as we headed north. We parted company at Winnipeg, Pat taking the food, beer, and what was left of our folding money, and heading west. I pocketed twenty-five cents and hitch-hiked east to Kenora.

12: The Stickpin

This particular incident occurred many years ago, but I thought it quite remarkable at the time, and I still do. Like a speck in a well, it floats up, and I look at it again to reassess its importance. Indomitable little Percy, one of the interesting people the Creator arranged for me to know, is a good object lesson for anyone, and here is why.

In 1957 or 1958, when Percy was past eighty, he was spending his declining years in a comfortable log cabin on the property of a friend, on the shore of Lake of the Woods. In the dead of winter not many people came to see him. As a lowly law student, I was visiting him to discuss his will, which my principal was in the process of revising. Percy had been a prospector, and I sensed that he had led an exciting and adventurous life and probably had some interesting tales to tell. On this bitter cold evening I asked him about how he acquired his enormous diamond and ruby studded stickpin. It was like opening a tap, and the story just poured out.

From time to time Percy would chunk the fire, and I would pour some tea into our mugs. Wood fires and tea and the spinning of yarns seem to go together on a cold night. As we put our feet up on the oven door of the ancient cast iron and chrome wood stove, he began his story.

Percy said the history of the pin went way back to a placer mining beach in Alaska when he was a very young man. As I figure it, the year would have been about 1900. He admitted that the pin was a dream even before that, when he was growing up on a hardscrabble farm somewhere in the Midwestern United States. Percy was a reader, and lurid magazine stories about gunslingers and gamblers often described the adventurers as fancy dressers replete with gold cuff links and diamond stickpins. Diamond stickpins became a symbol of affluence for the boy, and he vowed he would have one when he grew up and struck it rich. It was a long time before his fantasy was fulfilled, and then not quite in the way he had planned.

As Percy told it the Alaska mining camps were wild and woolly and totally lawless. The nearest thing to law and order were the vigilante groups called Miners Courts that would try to mediate serious disputes between individuals. The court would sometimes arrest a dangerous offender, perhaps a violent thief or a claim jumper, and chuck him into a wooden stockade until the next ship came by heading for Seattle or 'Frisco. The captains were usually good about taking troublemakers away in irons and releasing them when they reached the continental United States.

The law as it was known in Canada and the neighboring states to the south simply did not exist on the Alaskan beaches. In Percy's beach community you were expected to stay out of trouble, but if someone did you wrong you had to take your own vengeance or forget it.

Several shabby tent hotels and taverns lined the black sand beach, which I think must have been near what we now know as Nome. They had wooden bunks you could rent if you were desperate for a place to lay your head and were not too fastidious, and were willing to take a chance on picking up little critters left by the last occupant. Most men had their own tents up in the trees. But the tent hotels were all things to all men, offering booze, cookeries, dormitories, gambling tables, and entertainment. Everyone used them for one purpose or another. The meals were fish or moose meat, always with potatoes, never with vegetables. There were a number of haggard women around to keep a lonesome man company, provided he had a little cash, or dust. Everything was for sale, but the really big business was booze.

Fortunes were made in slaking the miners' thirsts. The hotels, as they were euphemistically called, got Kentucky bourbon in by the cask, and it came in two grades — terrible and merely bad. Sometimes the bartenders would spin out the bourbon with a form of vodka distilled back in the bush from sugar water and potato squeezings.

Percy was just a little guy, maybe five foot two and 110 pounds. He admitted he didn't go looking for trouble. Nevertheless, the adventure novels of the day intrigued him, and he determined on a life of excitement. In order to prepare for this new life he practiced endlessly with both a revolver and a rifle. Eventually he left the unproductive farm his father ran and headed for Seattle, which had the reputation of being rough and tough. A Seattle shooting gallery became his second home, and before long he became quick and accurate with both his guns.

The Alaska gold rush was big news in Seattle, and it was inevitable that Percy would ship out to try his luck on the beaches. With his .44-40 carbine and his six-gun (they actually called them that) he felt he was a match for anyone. Perhaps it was someone like Percy who originated the phrase "Smith and Wesson have made all men the same size."

The trip up the coast on the old sailing ship with auxiliary steam power was anything but luxurious, but the hundred or so young men and a few young women didn't mind it. Like Percy, they were filled with the spirit of adventure and most of them, including the women, carried guns. Every afternoon they ran shooting contests on the after deck.

Percy was mighty handy with a gun, but it didn't take him long to learn that a few people were as good as he was. This bothered him, because he had visualized himself as cock of the walk. Little self-doubts began to creep in. He had not been many days on his chosen beach when he discovered something that turned his little doubts into big doubts. He discovered that he just didn't have the will to be a killer. Gunfights had been an early teen-age fantasy. He put notions of being a feared gunslinger out of his mind when faced with the reality of survival in a man's world, figuring out all by himself that violence begets violence.

When I suggested that perhaps his midwestern farm upbringing had created in him a moral man who simply thought it was wrong to kill, he just snorted. He didn't answer right away, but took time to poke up the fire. I thought maybe the question had riled him, but he was just taking his time about answering. I halfway concluded that he hadn't thought about the matter very much in the last sixty years. I expected he might tell me he was really a bad fellow at heart, and that moral conviction played no part in his decision not to live by the gun. For some perverse reason many men, and women too, want to be thought of as wicked, I suppose because they think it is sissy to be good. But I had underestimated Percy. He had done many things and had many adventures in his lifetime, and he just didn't feel he had to prove anything to me or anyone else. Besides, at eighty you see things pretty clearly, and I suppose he hoped I would respect him as much for being truthful at eighty, as I would have for being a bad dude gunslinger at nineteen. And I did, too.

Anyway, Percy said there wasn't as much skullduggery and killing going on at the beaches as writers of the penny dreadfuls would have their readers believe. For the most part you didn't have to shoot someone to make a point. The majority of people on the beach felt the same way, and real gunfights seldom occurred. Even so, people respected a man who was a good shot. Percy explained with a twinkle of the eye and a great jiggling of the tie pin on his round little belly that signified mirth, that he was not fool enough to leave his gun behind, he just didn't pretend to be eager to draw it. He wore his gun the same way you behave with a dangerous dog — you don't look it in the eye or deliberately provoke it. He kept his revolver out of sight under a long coattail where it would not have the effect of challenging or provoking anyone. Once a week he would walk a long way from the beach and practice shooting, just so he would stay good. Just in case.

Percy's particular pal was a fellow named Sid, from back east somewhere. Last names were not used on the beach because many of the men did not want too much known about them. Sid was the head bartender at one of the less sleazy establishments. They sold booze, rented gambling tables, provided meals and beds and allowed girls to solicit business on the premises. What made the outfit marginally less sleazy than some of the other joints was that they didn't allow the whores to actually lay their customers in the bar, but rented small individual tents for the purpose of assignations. Their customers were a slightly better class of men.

A lot of money came in and most of it passed through Sid's hands. He kept it in a locked steel box under the corner of the rough wooden bar. For a small fee he would keep a prospector's poke in the box too. Everyone liked Sid because he was honest, and no down-on-his-luck prospector or starving greenhorn ever went out of the place hungry.

Occasionally Percy would relieve Sid or one of the other bartenders at the bar during the afternoon when it was quiet, but Sid always wanted to run the place himself in the evening. On days when there had been a good take Percy would wait with Sid until the tent was empty, standing guard while Sid counted the cash and put the padlock on the box. Like many a greenhorn Percy had not been able to pan enough gold to keep food in his belly, but he managed to survive by his wits and by doing odd jobs for Sid. He used to tell Sid that he would get off the beach when he had enough money to buy himself a diamond stickpin. They would both laugh about it because they knew it was an impossible dream.

That is the way matters stood when a northbound ship lightered in a gang of tenderfeet, most of whom were convinced they were going to strike it rich panning gold on the beach. Many of them flaunted revolvers and thought they were hot stuff. The captain of the ship sent word with the bo's'n that he would be returning southbound in a week or so, and passengers should be waiting on the beach.

One of the men who got off was no greenhorn, as he was familiar with how the tent hotels operated, having been on the beaches before. Like all the others he planned to strike it rich, but not by panning gold. He was called Buntline Blackie because of his dark visage and the long barreled .32-caliber Buntline Special revolver he carried, not that Percy knew his name while he was alive. His gun didn't throw a big slug, but it threw a small one with deadly accuracy. In its day it was widely held to be a fearsome weapon.

Buntline Blackie knew he wasn't going to pan any gold. Before he ever hit the beach he had plans to hold up one of the tent hotels, or taverns. He had grown a beard and changed his hat style while aboard ship, and he relied on this to protect him from recognition by anyone who may have seen him on other beaches. As he prowled the beach during the day he kept his hat pulled down over his eyes. Judging by the equipment they later found in his pack he must have planned to carry out the holdup, then disappear into the interior and live rough until the next southbound ship came along.

Blackie stalked the tent village like a nervous cat, trying as much as possible not to call attention to himself. He made an excuse to go into each of the canvas taverns to look around, searching out such things as trails to outhouses, rear entrances, and spy holes in the canvas. In particular he tried to memorize the locations of the miners' diggings so he could pick his way through them in the bush that night. He wasn't very smart, because in spite of his efforts at anonymity several people noticed him poking about the village, and commented on it the next day. Of course they said they knew he was up to no good, but by then it was too late to do anything about it.

It didn't take Blackie long to size up Sid's joint as yielding the best chance of easy pickings.

There were several holes in the tent through which any interested person could look, and he no doubt kept his eye on Sid throughout the evening. Percy was there too, but Blackie may not have noticed him sitting in a corner minding his own business. Blackie felt more comfortable when darkness fell. Eventually he was able to deduce that Sid was putting money into a strongbox behind the bar. Sid did not appear to be carrying iron, but Blackie could not tell if there was a gun hidden out of sight somewhere. He made up his mind that Sid's bar would be his target, and if Sid made a bad move he would shoot him down like a dog.

Sid's bar, like all the others, did a roaring business that day because of the influx of newcomers, so Sid stayed open late. The tables were full of shouting men in various stages of drunkenness, and the whiskey flowed like buttermilk. From his vantage point at a peephole Blackie watched with avarice as Sid made numerous trips to the strong box.

In the wee hours the place began to empty out. Men stomped out into the blackness, took a leak, and stumbled off to their tents. Only Sid and Percy and a few drunks remained in the bar. Percy thought later that Blackie simply hadn't seen him, or believed he was too insignificant to be a threat.

Blackie watched and waited. When Sid began to count the money he made his move. Striding in through the door of the tent with his wicked gun in his hand he shouted, "Everybody put your hands up where I can see them. You, Barkeep, open that box under the bar or I'll blow your head open." His voice had just the hint of a tremor in it, which Percy noted with misgiving. Sid stood rigid. The sawed-off, two-hole, 12-gauge shotgun that he kept behind the bar was just out of reach, but he knew all about the accuracy of the Buntline Special, and he dared not move.

From where he was sitting Percy could sense the holdup man's nervousness. He knew it was time to act or his friend would die by the hand of the stranger. He was aghast. It was time to do what he had trained himself to do and he dreaded it. Fear, repugnance and his Midwest farm boy conscience all obscured his will at the same time, perhaps slowing him down an iota. He felt sick, but concern for his friend and his long hours of practice paid off.

Percy did what he had to do. His hand flew down to the holster under his coattail. Without rising he drew his gun and drilled Blackie right through his elbow, shattering the bone.

Just as Blackie was about to pull the trigger on Sid he heard the roar of Percy's gun. The bullet struck him just in time to deflect his aim. Intending to hit Sid in the head, he instead hit him in the forearm. Blackie did not go down, but stood there in the gloom of the tent in a state of shock, peering sideways at Percy in disbelief, trying to shift his gun to his other hand.

Percy shot him again, right between the eyes, and the Buntline Special went scuttling away across the dirt floor.

Sid was grievously wounded, but not finished. As the bullet that was intended to send him into the next world entered his arm, he reached for his shotgun with his remaining arm. He swung awkwardly on Blackie and — just an instant after Percy's second shot hit Blackie — Sid pulled both triggers. The shots went wild, but it didn't matter, because Blackie was already dead. Sid would have been dead too, if the Buntline Special had been of a larger caliber.

Bartenders materialized and curiosity seekers pressed in, all wanting to congratulate Percy and tell him what a fine fellow he was. A couple of drunks dragged Blackie out by the heels, leaving him in the dirt.

Sid was in a bad way, bleeding heavily from a severed artery in his bullet-mangled arm. He was certain to be a goner if his friends didn't act fast. By dint of much gun waving and shouting Percy managed to clear the tent of drunks and hangers-on, and with a group of friends he set to work on Sid.

The first order of business was a tourniquet to stop the bleeding.

Cutting off Sid's shirt and sweater, they tied a strip around his arm just below the elbow, above the wound. Sid passed in and out of consciousness, screaming and sobbing incoherently. Fighting to hold him steady, they flopped him up on the bar. A dozen coal oil lamps were clustered in such a way as to throw light on the patient. Sid finally had to be tied down to keep him from further injuring himself.

Whiskey from behind the bar was used as a sterilizing agent, an anesthetic for Sid, and to impart Dutch courage to his handlers. Unwanted people pressed in again, but the stench of coal oil, bad whiskey, vomit and blood soon drove all but the hardiest out into the cool fresh air of the night. Pouring whiskey into Sid and each other, the amateur surgeons steeled themselves for what they had to do. It was a relief when Sid finally went limp and quiet.

A carpenter's saw and a sharp knife were brought over from the cook tent, and the amputation began. Sterilization and libation were again by cheap Kentucky bourbon. Five minutes of cutting and hacking found the forearm and hand of Sid on the floor along with the vomit and blood. It was a gruesome moment, and sixty years later Percy's nose wrinkled in distaste as he told me about it.

Sid's life was saved, but at a terrible cost in suffering. He was so low from shock and loss of blood that he could only nod his thanks to his friends. A few days later when a southbound steamer appeared, Percy retrieved Sid's money and gold from its hiding place under the plank floor in Sid's sleeping tent, tying it in a rawhide bag around Sid's waist. He was able to purchase a first-class passage to Seattle for his friend, and he paid a returning dance hall girl to nurse him for the seven-day trip.

The miners made him drag Blackie's body into the bush behind the camp and bury it without a funeral. Percy told me ruefully that he grew up that night on the beach. He saved one man's life and ended another's.

Taking Sid's place at the bar, Percy saved his money, and as soon as he had a nest egg he hauled out for Seattle. He was devastated to find that Sid had already moved on. Asking questions and writing letters turned up nothing, as Sid had simply vanished. Percy still didn't have his diamond stickpin.

Ten years passed before Percy saw Sid again.

Hard work was not to Percy's liking, but neither was starving or stealing, so he worked as a prospector when he had to. Occasionally he was able to make a lot of money, and he lived well while it lasted. Gambling was his passion, but never an addiction, and he would hit a different gambling joint every time he went on a spree. Hoping to find a mother lode of riches, as gamblers and prospectors do, he became well known in the pleasure resorts of the west coast. It was in a gambling den in San Francisco that he met Sid again.

People seemed to be gathering around a particular table and spending a lot of money, so Percy drifted over to see what was going on. The game was blackjack. He placed a bet, and even though his cards weren't great he won. Glancing up at the dealer he found himself looking at the face of Sid, he of the amputated arm on the black sand beach in Alaska. Percy's eyes lit up in recognition. It was on the tip of his tongue to greet his old friend when Sid gave a barely perceptible shake of his head. Saying nothing, Percy bet again, heavily.

The one armed dealer flipped the cards with speed and wonderful precision, and Percy knew why the gamblers were attracted to his table. "Fifteen. Eighteen. Nineteen. Twenty-one." Percy won again.

Percy didn't press his luck at the table all at once. He had not exchanged a single word with the dealer, but the volume of chips in his pocket told him there was more than just ordinary luck running in his favor. From time to time he would work his way back to Sid's table, and if there was a new crowd of players he would join in a hand or two. He lost when he bet small, but he often won when he bet big.

By two o'clock in the morning Percy had the whacking great sum of $3,000 in chips in his pocket, a fortune in that day. Pressing through the crowd, he found Sid at his elbow, whispering out of the side of his mouth. "It's time to cash in and leave, friend. If you stay around the security man will get suspicious. Adios." And he was gone.

In the morning Percy went to a jewelry store and spent a bundle on the biggest diamond stickpin in the place. Returning to Sid's table in the evening, he didn't place any bets, but watched for a while, and flashed his pin. Sid looked up and smiled. Percy went on his way.

Percy never saw Sid again. Half a century later he still had the pin, which he wore in a broad tie reminiscent of the cravats of an earlier time.

As I walked out into the frosty night I looked back at the chimney on the old log cabin, and saw a shower of sparks rising to the sky. I knew Percy was putting the fire in the wood stove to bed for the night. It suddenly struck me that we had not said a word about his will.

I have often wondered if Percy's story was true. I was only a law student at the time, and not as adept at detecting falsehood as I became later in my career. But I have had a good many years to think about it, and my conclusion is that the stickpin story is the truth, and it happened just as Percy said it did.

13: The Northern Health Service Carries On

Barry Jorgenson was a good friend and neighbor with whom I shared a glass from time to time, back on Coney Island in Kenora. He was a civil engineer, and sometimes a builder of houses, but he preferred bush flying in the north because it brought him in contact with interesting people.

Regularly every Wednesday morning in the winter he would fire up his employer's cantankerous Cessna 180 and fly down to Northwest Angle, a reserve right on the Minnesota border. It was hardly what you might call a northern reserve, but it was as difficult to access as any in the far north. If one were to drive there one would have to drive fifty miles west of Kenora on the Trans-Canada Highway into Manitoba, then drive forty miles south on a gravel road into the State of Minnesota, then bounce around bush roads back in a more or less northerly direction to the Northwest Angle of Lake of the Woods, which was part of an ancient fur trade route to the west. There on the north bank was a squalid little settlement that held a mixture of very fine people and others that nature seemed to have short-changed. I use the word "nature" in preference to other words that come to mind because I am reluctant to get into a discussion of the function of the deity in these matters, but the fact is that misery and desolation seemed to be the lot of many of the people at that reserve. It was always a source of wonder to me that a place like this could throw up such good people alongside the more unfortunate ones.

In order to start an airplane on a winter morning you have to pour in warm oil, heat the engine with a Herman Nelson construction heater or a blowpot, swing the prop by hand in order to loosen it up, then press the button. If you have done everything right, the engine just might start.

On a particular morning in the 1980s Barry managed to start the engine and headed off through the ice crystals, a feature of particularly cold days in the frozen north. A twenty-minute flight over Lake of the Woods brought him to the airstrip on the ice that ran between Magnusson Island on the American side and the village of Northwest Angle. Waiting for Barry on the ice was a small group of people, including three women

Kenora and Coney Island, Ontario, c. 1950.

B.J. was to fly to Kenora for medical appointments, and the lady from the store on Magnusson Island.

I have to tell you about her, even though it does not really form part of the story. This lady ran a small tourist resort in the summer, she was the postmistress for the little post office that served both the American side and the Canadian side, she was a deputy conservation officer for the State of Minnesota, and she would open her bar if a thirsty traveler demanded it. It should not be necessary to point out that if a traveler managed to make it all the way to Magnusson Island...well, I am sure you get the picture. The little bar was a popular place. The really important thing about her was that she was a qualified nurse, and the Northern Health Services paid her to be their representative at Northwest Angle just half a mile across the border on the Canadian side.

No one paid any attention to the fact of an international boundary. I visited the area myself in both winter and summer and observed the casual manner in which the local Indians and the Minnesota Swedes crossed back and forth, the nearest official crossing point being many miles away. In fact just to test out the friendly border I once went by boat to Northwest Angle, crossed to the American side, discussed an assault that had occurred in Canada with the nurse, bought a child's toy in her store, and had a drink in the little bar, all without encountering any official on either side, other than the lady herself.

The arrangement was that the Magnusson Island lady would select the three people who most needed medical attention and send them in to Kenora on B.J.'s usual Wednesday morning medical run. B.J., or the hospital, would see that they got to a doctor's office, and at the end of the day they would fly back to Northwest Angle in B.J.'s drafty Cessna.

On the day in question B.J. picked up his three ladies and a note from the nurse in the usual way, dropping them off on the ice in Kenora where someone from the hospital awaited. Then he jumped into his own vehicle and drove straight to my office.

Barry stormed in emitting oaths and clouds of steam from his clothing. He was clearly in a state of high dudgeon. In between stomping his feet and rubbing his ears to restore the circulation he told his story.

"I made my regular Northwest Angle run this morning, and as I pulled up to the group on the ice I recognized an old lady I had flown in several times before. I could see her arm was in a sling, so I took her other elbow to help her up into the cockpit. She winced, but did not cry out, and I realized I had hurt her.

'Didn't I fly you out just a few weeks ago with a broken arm?'

'Yes, but this time he has broke the other arm,' she said with difficulty."

Barry went on, his voice quivering with indignation. "I didn't need to be told the "he" she referred to was her husband. I asked her anyway, and she nodded yes without looking at me. When I finally got a look at her I could see bruising about her face and eyes. I asked if her husband had done that, too, and she would only look down without answering. I tell you, I was so God damn angry I botched the landing back in Kenora and shook the poor old lady up again."

Lucy came in with a cup of coffee for B.J. and tea for me. He paused for a moment to sip, and continued. "There was a nurse from the hospital waiting on the ice in Kenora and I told her all about it. She drove away with her patients, saying she was pretty sure the old lady would refuse to make any complaint, as such beatings were commonplace, but she would notify the OPP (Ontario Provincial Police) about it in hopes that something would be done."

Barry ran out of steam, and I promised I would follow the case closely. He flew the old lady and her fellow patients back to the reserve later in the afternoon. This time she had both arms in casts.

I later confirmed with the police that there had never been a report of violence to the old lady. It simply was not in the culture of the people to complain about such things, and getting witnesses to give evidence was practically impossible, as I knew from sad experience.

There was no trial, of course. The OPP sent in an experienced male constable and a sympathetic young female constable, but the old lady refused to make any complaint. Local support for her was conspicuously absent. Nevertheless the officers would have taken her back out to a shelter in town if she had been willing to come. When the lady constable made her report she said that the old lady's only comment was that she had suffered abuse at the hands of her husband all their life together, and she guessed that she would stay with him till the end.

Case closed. As a matter of fact, case never opened.

Incidents like this were, and still are, infuriating to conscientious authorities, including earnest young police officers and court officials. Barry Jorgenson was not constrained by the same protocol as are government people, and he made his displeasure known to all. We just had to sit by and let nature take its course in cases like this, often with sad consequences to the silent victims, who just withered away. It was not politically correct to say anything publicly that might be construed as a negative comment on the First Nations culture or way of life. Usually such cases never made it to the courtroom door, but if they did and the Crown attorney knew that the victim would not testify he would have to withdraw or otherwise call a halt to the prosecution. On these occasions it was tempting to say something derogatory about the way of life that supported, or at least covered up, family violence, but in the interest of retaining the good will of the Native people I was restrained in my comments.

I am pleased to say that family violence is not as prevalent as it once was on the reserves, but any is too much. To the uninitiated who would deny the proposition that violence is in any way cultural with the Native people, I can only say that if it is not cultural or traditional, there is a hell of a lot of it on Canada's northern reserves, and political correctness be damned. I have been contemplating this issue for thirty-five or forty years, and I think it is more important to maintain credibility and to speak the truth than to be popular. I say unequivocally that the race of First Nations people that inhabits the central part of the continent carries within itself the seeds of its own destruction as long as it tolerates domestic abuse and sexual molestation in the way that is still so prevalent today. I refuse to be told that it is unacceptable for the law to meddle in cultural or traditional matters, and every time there is a denial or a cover-up the race is diminished. B.J. was right to be upset by what happened to his little old lady.

I said some of these things in an editorial printed over five issues in *Wawatay News,* thinking it might have an impact with First Nations people, but if I am to judge by the feedback it was largely ignored, the exception being a very few remarks from white wannabe-Native supporters to the effect that I should mind my own business, and quit interfering. What little praise there was came from some of the First Nations leaders. The editorial was as a result of more than thirty years as a Crown attorney, many visits to Northern reserves, countless contacts with pilots, police, missionaries, contacts with the genuine leaders that are emerging, and many years spent working alongside Ojibway and Cree Indians as a boy and young man. This editorial appears as a chapter at the end of this book.

I didn't really try deliberately to mount a soapbox when something jogged my memory of B.J.'s story, but I must admit that the injection of a little passion benefits both the cause and the narrative. Perhaps I am just a natural born interferer.

14: The Man in Row 20

The old man sat slumped on the left side of the DC-8, next to the window. He had taken too much to drink the night before and felt dreadful. He fidgeted with his collar to loosen it, but his ingrained sense of propriety was such that he did not take his tie off altogether. He was a decent man, and did not cheat on his wife when he was away on business, and now he wished with all his heart that the trip was over. In forty-five minutes the aircraft would be on the ground in Winnipeg, and soon after that he would be home. He would remove his shoes and tie and his wife would bring him a nice cup of tea.

The heat in the cabin was becoming oppressive. He ran his finger around inside his collar again, but left his tie on.

He instinctively disliked the woman sitting in the seat next to him. She wore too much makeup on her jowly face, and her hair was colored a garish blue. She talked too much and too loudly to the man on the aisle, and wouldn't pass things on to the man at the window to make it easier for the stewardess. For some reason the perfume the woman was wearing assailed his senses, and he thought that must be what was making him ill. Through a fog of discomfort he reflected that she probably thought that he was a nobody. As it happened, the man beside her on the aisle was her husband, and he did not like her either.

No one noticed when the man in the window seat half rose to his feet and was immediately jerked back by his loose seat belt. He wanted to tell someone that something was dreadfully wrong inside his chest, but the pain was snatching his voice, and he felt himself sinking into darkness. The painted lady may have noticed that he was flopped forward with his head against the back of the seat ahead, but if she did she gave no indication of it.

When the stewardess passed by she noticed the strange position of the window seat passenger, and leaned over to talk to him. The man on the aisle pulled his knees in to be accommodating, but the painted lady stiffened and refused to be cooperative. As I watched from the other side of the aisle, I began to hate her.

"Sir," said the stewardess. Then a little louder, "Sir, are you all right? Would you look at me please?"

With a visible effort of will the passenger turned his face to the concerned young woman. It was contorted and blue. The stewardess whispered out loud, "My God!" as she made the oxygen sign to another stewardess a little further up the aisle. Almost immediately she was there with a green metal bottle from which dangled a tube and a mask. The first stewardess struggled by the other passengers, clapping the mask over the heart victim's face, and opened the valve. By this time all the nearby passengers were looking, caught up in the drama of the moment. The painted lady's husband stood in the aisle pulling at her arm, but she was clearly reluctant to move.

Faintly, through the electronic fog, the passengers heard the P.A. system: "Is there a doctor aboard, please? Is there a doctor aboard? We have a medical emergency. If there is a doctor aboard would he please go to row 20?"

In no time a spry old gentleman appeared. He was about the same age as the heart attack victim, but his self-assured movements and his pink complexion were in direct contrast. "Move quickly, please," he said to the three people in row 19 ahead of the patient, but they were already moving out. He put the seat backs down and crawled over them to get to the man next to the window. Still obdurate, the painted lady was being tugged at by her husband and the stewardess. She was being deliberately slow. The doctor did not bother speaking to her, but grabbed her by her fleshy upper arm and jerked her out of her seat. The stewardess raised the chair arms in row 20 to make a bed, three seats wide, for the sick man, who flopped down like a rag doll, knowing nothing.

The doctor had only his skill and his two hands, no little black bag and no magic medicine. Rolling the patient on his back, he ripped open the man's shirt by sliding his finger up the row of buttons and sending them whirring away like flies. Someone produced a jackknife to cut the tie off.

The ghastly blue face stared up uncomprehendingly as the doctor half straddled his patient, slamming his fist into his chest time and time again, hard. To the untrained observer it looked like mayhem without a purpose. Pausing from time to time he would lean over and put his ear to the patient's chest, then he would sit up and resume thumping. The watchers winced with every blow. The stewardess attempted, without much success, to get oxygen into the patient. Hope began to fade.

Suddenly the man's hand flew up to his throat, causing those passengers who could see to give a spontaneous cheer. The cheer communicated itself to the other passengers, who all broke out into happy conversation. Positioning the mask more firmly, the doctor leaned down and listened again. When he looked up he was smiling. The closer passengers could see the patient's eyelids fluttering, his complexion pinking. Even the passengers not close enough to see somehow understood that a miracle had occurred in their midst.

On the ground a medical team was waiting by the runway. They carried the patient out, and as he passed the stewardesses he lifted his hand.

A close observer would have noticed that the doctor was weary as he made his way back to his own seat. Following him was an Air Canada official with a pad of paper and a pen, saying something in an urgent voice. As he passed up the aisle one could quite clearly hear the doctor say, "No, you do not need to have my name. No, I don't give a damn about your records. Look here, if you absolutely must write something about it, just say that a country doctor saw his duty and did it."

I felt good on the drive back to Kenora.

15: About Annie O'Ryan

I guess I have known about Annie O'Ryan just about forever. Or at least it seems like it from the perspective of a man who has completed his seventh decade and still remembers all his father's best stories.

Pop sort of had Annie on a pedestal, because she could always tell when a man had a good thirst on, and she always had near-to-hand the means of quenching that thirst. In the 1920s many young men were pilots or railroaders in Sioux Lookout, and as such it just stands to reason that they had a powerful thirst a fair percentage of the time. There were only a handful of policemen between The Lakehead and the Manitoba border, and they did not trouble people like Annie, who were looked upon as public benefactors. Business was brisk for Annie, who, with her husband, ran a sort of rooming-house hotel, and sold booze out of one of the upstairs rooms.

"Come and get it, boys," she would say. "Here it is in a warm glass, just twenty-five cents a shot." This was at a time when liquor was purchased by prescription at the pharmacy for two dollars a bottle. She would flip a shot glass out of her ample bosom, fill it to the brim with whiskey, and collect a quarter. Pop thought this was hilarious and told the story with gusto till the day he died. Evidently all the other young pilots thought it was hilarious too, and Annie's place was a favorite destination after a day's flying or a hard run on the railroad. It may have been Annie's personality, or the hope of a peek at her boobs, or the whiskey, but whatever it was it made a lot of quarters for Annie. Enough, it was said, to pay off the mortgage on her hotel well before maturity.

More than half a lifetime later I was present in Sioux Lookout during a time of great need when an old policeman sent a junior policeman out for a jug of whiskey. "Go to that old hotel down the street. Go up the stairs to the second floor and knock on the door of room 27. A lady with big — you know…" (A gesture of the hands here, palms cupped inwards towards the chest. After all, the old inspector had a certain sense of propriety.) "will answer the door. Tell her you want a bottle of good whiskey. Tell her it's for me, and she won't charge you anything."

"I can't do that, Sir. I'm in uniform. She'd never give me a bottle anyway. What if the boys at the local detachment saw me?" The young constable was dancing up and down in agony. Perhaps it was because his feet were cold, or perhaps it was because he had to relieve himself, but more than likely it was because he was agitated by the rather unconventional order of his superior officer.

The inspector was unperturbed. "Don't raise petty objections, Lad. Just do it." And he sent the constable out into the winter air, which was scarcely colder than the frozen-up hotel room we happened to be in at the time. Privately I thought the young officer had made several good points, but I didn't want to rock the boat by saying so, as it might have cast a pall over my main mission, which was to persuade the attorney general of the province of Ontario to hire me as a Crown attorney. It was his hotel room we happened to be in at the time.

In due course the officer was back. "Holy shit, Sir, she actually did it. She gave me a bottle of Canadian Club," and he produced it from under his great coat. He almost made the mistake of giggling. The inspector unscrewed the cap and tossed it at the wastebasket. Respectful silence prevailed while we all took a snort from the bottle. The officer, as junior man present, was the last to take a pull at the bottle, and he downed three fingers at a gulp, thinking the old inspector might cut him off at any moment. He didn't know the inspector very well.

The honorable attorney general took another swig, and then set about the serious business of interviewing me from his bed, on which he lay fully dressed. We talked about politics for a while, and he satisfied himself that I would not undermine him, even though we did not share the same political affiliation. We talked about aviation, and he told a story about peeing off the float of a plane that had landed in the middle of Hudson Bay. It seems that he made the mistake of facing into the wind. It wasn't very funny, but I laughed anyway. We talked about mining and prospecting for a while.

Even for that day, when unstructured interviews were common, it was an odd way to go about getting a job. Anyway, he looked at his deputy, Bill Common, who just nodded and reached for the bottle. He said I could move into the courthouse in Kenora as soon as I was ready. I wondered for years whether it was because of the whiskey, or because I laughed at his story about peeing into the wind from the float of the plane. Not long before he died, my father told me he and the honorable gentleman had been partners in a little mining syndicate in the territories thirty years previously.

When I got back to Kenora I told my dad about the day's activities. He said nothing about his old connection with the attorney general, but he repeated the story I had heard many times about the lady with the warm shot glass, and this time he put a name to her. It was Annie O'Ryan. Pop told me I should visit the lady myself sometime, and see what developed. I did, and the visit was fruitful. The lady, quite elderly by this time, poured me a stiff one. She took no money, and I didn't see where the glass came from, but I could imagine, I could imagine…

But that's not the end of the story. Another half lifetime later, long after I had retired, I was at Lansdowne House doing some prosecutions for the new Crown attorney. I was in the police office adjacent to the local airport when an attractive young woman swaggered in and threw her pack on the floor. You can always tell the real northerners by the way they sling their packs. I looked her over closely. Interesting. I may have smiled. She caught me looking at her, and glared at me. "Who the hell is he?" she said to the local cop, jerking her thumb in my direction.

Now I like a woman with a little "piss and vinegar" in her blood, and I set about smoothing her feathers and getting to know her. Almost everyone in the North is from somewhere else, and I was surprised to learn that she was from Sioux Lookout, a mere couple of hundred miles away. Just around the corner, so to speak. She left Sioux to get an education, and later returned to become a probation officer, and was attending the same court that had brought me to Lansdowne. Her name was O'Ryan, and her family had been in the hotel business.

"Wait a minute," I exclaimed. "Was one of your ancestors a sweet old lady who lived on the second floor of O'Ryan's Hotel and sold…"

"…whiskey at a quarter a shot," she filled in with a big grin. "Yes, that was Granny. The family used to deny it had ever been so, but she was so well known that we just gave up."

And that's how we get to know people in the north.

16: A Tough Cop

It would be a mistake to think that Chief Jack Pike was just another hard-bitten old dinosaur, a holdover from an age when police were supposed to be tough guys and not much else. He was a tough guy all right, but make no mistake about it, there was a lot more to him than that.

Chief Pike was still a formidable man when he was past sixty. He had been a boxer in his youth, and in 1954 people who were less than charitable said that the reason he held his job was that he could lick all the miscreants in town, as well as his own men, if necessary. All except Sergeant Fred Whitehead, of course, but those two old bulls had no necessity to try each other on. No one ever dared to call Chief Pike anything but "Chief" except for his wife Ida and his fishing pal, lawyer L.A. McLennan, QC, later judge of the District Court.

I don't want to be taking anything away from the Chief's intellectual attainments, for he was a fine all-round police officer, but one of the old school. By this I mean that he had no objection if Sergeant Whitehead wanted to kick some young lad's butt instead of dragging him before the austere Magistrate Wolfe, or to spank an errant lassie with his huge hand, through her dress, of course. It was well known that the Chief was an expert at meting out such discipline himself. Such was the temper of the times, and of the community, that the citizenry approved of this type of discipline.

I wasn't raised in Kenora, not coming on the scene as a fixture until I articled to Jack Doner in 1957. This was in the days before the world of lawyers and police was so sharply divided into "them and us." I got to know most of the young police officers, and they had many tales to tell of the prowess of the Chief and his sergeant. They all admired the two old bulls, but unfortunately they didn't exercise the same discretion in their own dealings with the public, and a few of them attracted an unbecoming reputation for being too rough on citizens who didn't deserve it.

Ida Pike, who used to baby-sit my young'uns, would tell me tales about how her Jack kept law and order at Goldpines, a staging site for the Red Lake gold camps during the 1920s and '30s, when there wasn't another policeman to back him up closer than seventy-five air miles away. When Jack went in to Goldpines as one of the earliest OPP constables his instructions were simple — he was to "keep order and not hurt anyone too bad." It would have been considered highly inconvenient if he ever had to lay a charge. He carried out his mandate with his dukes, of course.

Ida's stories about the Goldpines days were kept alive by Ron and Bunty Nicols, an expatriate English couple who had lived in Goldpines during the rough and tumble days, and retired to the nearby Hydro project at Ear Falls when Goldpines shut down. If Ron had had money he would have been called a remittance man, but as it was he had to work for a living. Ron did not particularly like Jack Pike, however he admired him, if I might be permitted the distinction. I mention this simply because I want you to know that Ron had no reason to puff up the Jack Pike stories. He said it was wise to keep clear of Jack Pike when he was in his peacekeeping mode. In an unguarded moment Bunty hinted that Jack had once knocked Ron about rather severely when he caught him in a minor peccadillo.

Ida told me that in the Goldpines days she would sew Jack into a pair of tight leather gloves before he left the house on Saturday night. She would then either have a few honest women in to spend the evening with her, or retire to the local hotel, which was run by Ron Nicols. A sort of a protective herd instinct, if you have ever read anything about the buffalo in the Old West. Goldpines was that sort of a place. And Jack would roam the boardwalks and paths exacting obeisance from anyone who he suspected might have bad intentions, such a state of mind being purely a subjective judgment by Jack. For two years Jack was "cock of the walk" until he transferred to the Kenora Town Police Force, where he eventually became chief.

I guess you'd say that Jack Pike was a real tough cop. Anyway, that was how the world viewed him in the 1960s, and that was how he wanted it. He took pains to ensure that people continued to think that way even after the Keewatin Bank Robbery, I suppose because it was easier to keep people in line if they thought he was a mean son-of-a-bitch. The truth is that this stern, autocratic man had a soft spot, which didn't fit his carefully nurtured image.

At the time of the robbery in 1954, Kenora and its smaller sibling, Keewatin, were just tiny enclaves of civilization on the winding, narrow Trans-Canada Highway. It was a simple matter to seal the area off and to watch the nearby railway stations at train time. It was definitely not a prime location for heavy-duty crime. Staging a bank holdup in Keewatin was really a dumb thing to do, but that is exactly what a man and a young woman did on Tuesday the 21st of September 1954, although not very successfully, as it turned out.

Police forces don't operate like they used to. Today we read about serious crimes occurring in one location while the police right next door are deliberately kept in ignorance of developments, I suppose to ensure that no one will sneak in to hog the glory of a spectacular arrest in a high-profile case. But it wasn't that way in rural Canada in 1954, when co-operation was the way to go. Before the case was closed the Keewatin Police, the Kenora Police, the Winnipeg Police, the Ontario Provincial Police, the RCMP and the Canadian Pacific Railway Police were all involved.

I barely remember the incident as that was the year I got home from university, and I was much too busy chasing girls and trying to make a dollar to be concerned with local crime. But I have the newspaper reports, the memory of Jack Beckworth, who was the young chief constable in Keewatin, and a booklet about Kenora by Stu King, then the editor of the *Kenora Miner and News* and a lifelong friend of Bob MacGarva, an OPP constable of whom much has been written. I was not in any way on "the inside" of the mechanism of law and order at the time, so I do not know how the various police departments communicated, and who made the decisions, but in a crisis they always seemed to know what to do. When the Keewatin bank was robbed they operated like a well-oiled team and not, as might be expected today, like the Keystone Cops.

"This is a stickup. Get your hands in the air or get your head blown off!" are the words reported by *The Miner and News* to have been spoken by the bandit to James Rolston, the manager of the Royal Bank. Rolston and his employees handed over bundles containing almost $12,000 and the robber vanished in a waiting cab.

After a few blocks the gunman forced the cab driver out and took the wheel himself, leaving towards the West Highway, which led to Winnipeg. And then he disappeared — poof! Just like that. Soon afterwards the car was found abandoned just outside Keewatin.

The local police forces all gathered at the scene, roadblocks were set up, and the hunt was on. They even brought a police dog in from Winnipeg.

When the capture of the gunman was finally effected, Chief Pike was quick to assign credit to everyone who assisted. It was not until years later that he told how he had formulated a plan for the trap, and even then he modestly played his own part in low key.

Suspecting from the beginning that the lone robber had an accomplice, the Kenora–Keewatin police officers saw to it that the Winnipeg police were immediately notified. It was bad luck for Rhoda Milliard later in the day when an alert police officer and a curious car rental agent put their heads together, having heard of the events in Keewatin. They heard Rhoda asking for directions to Kenora from behind the wheel of the car she had just rented, ostensibly for pleasure driving around the city. The girl, for she was still very young, had a large sum of money in her possession. She refused to discuss the money or explain to the police where she had been in the previous forty-eight hours. There was, of course, no obligation for the girl to talk to the police, but it is a proposition of simple common sense that if you want people to think you have committed no offence you have to do your best to look innocent. The girl's refusal to talk to the policeman made her look guilty as sin. Under questioning she admitted nothing, but being sure of their quarry the police nevertheless returned her to Keewatin. She refused to give Pike or MacGarva or Beckworth any information whatsoever. She was lodged in the Kenora cells, but still refused to talk.

This is the point at which Jack Pike became vague about what happened. Rhoda appeared to be very loyal to her companion, the as yet undiscovered robber, and the betting was that she wouldn't spill the beans — but spill them she did, in private to Chief Pike. Rhoda told how she and her fiancé, Raymond Leonard Shultz, with whom she was desperately in love, had traveled from the West Coast and planned to rob a bank along the way. Rhoda, after the fashion of young girls in love, was not thinking too well, and later she said, somewhat ruefully, that she "hoped to reform" her lover after they were married. She admitted to being disillusioned by the slow and dusty bus ride across the prairies, and by the fleabag hotels they had to stay in. But Shultz promised her bright lights and money, and like country girls the world over she believed him. They were in love, and didn't that make everything all right?

Rhoda told Chief Pike that she waited in concealment until Shultz had got the money, and as he drove by he threw her a bundle for her own use. She was to make her way to Winnipeg, rent a car, drive back to a prearranged spot near Keewatin, pick up Shultz, then head right back to Winnipeg. There was only a half hour to go before Rhoda and Shultz were to make the meet. In the frantic moments preceding the big scoop no one thought to ask Chief Pike how he had managed to get Rhoda to talk, and even if they had, the chances were he wouldn't have said. As a matter of fact it was more than twenty years before the close-mouthed old Chief finally told what influenced Rhoda to be cooperative in the arrest of her lover.

Chief Pike was not in charge of the investigation, but Rhoda Milliard was in his lock-up, and he was the one who formulated the plan to nab Shultz, so all the others just sort of naturally went along with him. It was decided to proceed to the rendezvous in a car of a type specified by Rhoda, with Constable Bob MacGarva of the OPP at the wheel, decked out in a woman's hat, all according to Rhoda's directions. Chief Pike and Constable Stan Cox rode hunched down on the floor behind MacGarva. They headed down the Keewatin Beach Road, stopping just short of the spot to which Rhoda had directed them. Chief Pike and Constable Cox slipped quietly out of the car and hid in the bush beside the road as MacGarva cruised slowly up and down smoking a cigarette, all according to plan.

Suddenly a figure appeared out of the darkness on MacGarva's side of the car. Quickly crossing to the other side the man put his hand on the door. MacGarva bided his moment, and then leveled his gun and his flashlight at the man, backing him to the edge of the road. MacGarva took a loaded revolver from the man's pocket. It was Shultz, of course. He had risen up only a few feet from where Chief Pike had hidden himself in the leaves!

Ten days after the robbery Shultz and Milliard appeared before Magistrate Wolfe in Magistrate's Court, pleading guilty to charges arising out of the bank robbery. No one expected leniency for Shultz, and it was no surprise when he was sentenced to six years in the penitentiary for the holdup. What happened to Rhoda Milliard was, however, a complete surprise to everyone except hard-nosed old Chief Jack Pike, and perhaps to Rhoda's lawyer.

Rhoda's lawyer was L.A. McLennan, QC, who just happened to be a good friend of Chief Pike. A ripple of astonishment ran through the court room when lawyer McLennan announced that he was going to call Chief Pike to the stand to testify on Rhoda's behalf at the sentence hearing. After all, what could this stern purveyor of community order say on behalf of a woman who had helped rob a bank? Chief Pike said that he had been favorably impressed by the girl, who appeared to have an excellent upbringing, and was definitely out of character as a bank robber. He pointed out that it was only through her cooperation that a shootout was avoided. He added his recommendation to that of lawyer McLennan, in a plea in mitigation. The Chief admired Rhoda's loyalty to Shultz, even if it was misplaced, and having met Rhoda's parents, who had come east for the trial, he was convinced that she did not deserve a great penalty for her part in the robbery. Chief Beckworth of Keewatin had done his part by laying only a charge of possession of stolen goods as relating to the cash Shultz had thrown her, when he might have reaped a measure of glory by laying the much more serious charge of armed robbery. Magistrate Wolfe was thereby enabled to distinguish between Shultz and Rhoda for sentencing purposes.

Rhoda Milliard's sentence was almost a foregone conclusion. Magistrate Wolfe suspended the passing of sentence and put her on probation for two years, which was really just a kiss. But then it wasn't every day that Chief Pike came to court to put in a word for a criminal, either. Part of her conditions of probation was that she should return to British Columbia with her parents, be of good behavior, and regularly report to Magistrate Wolfe in writing. Within a year Rhoda Millard requested permission to be married, and the court released her from her probation.

Over the years people forgot that Rhoda had initially been totally non-communicative, and if anyone thought about it they probably ascribed the shift in loyalty to a wish by Rhoda to avoid a shootout, that being the official line handed out by Chief Pike at the time. I don't know why I probed that aspect of the case twenty years later, but this is what Chief Pike told me, almost under duress.

The Chief had many conversations with Rhoda, commencing with the drive back from Winnipeg. He found her to be intelligent, but utterly naive, a small town girl with very little experience of life. Believing her to have a well-developed sense of morality, he questioned her closely about her relationship with Raymond Shultz. His name was already known to them from hotel receipts, although not, of course, his location, and the Chief was puzzled about the hold Shultz exerted on her.

Once more the Chief looked through the luggage of Shultz and young Rhoda, hoping for inspiration. This time he noticed a discoloration on the lining of Shultz' suitcase, right along one edge. Using an old fashioned razor blade he carefully slit the lining exactly parallel to the line of discoloration, which turned out to be glue. Probing behind the cloth lining he brought out a marriage certificate indicting that Shultz already had a wife! Chief Pike knew instinctively that this piece of paper was going to have a profound effect on the case.

Chief Pike ordered the girl brought in and sat down in a chair across from him. Saying nothing, he slid Shultz' wedding certificate in front of her. Picking it up, she looked at it for a long moment before her face crumpled. She slid the paper back across the table. "All right, I'll tell you where he is," she whispered through her tears.

The time was just one half-hour before Rhoda Milliard was supposed to meet Raymond Shultz on the bush road outside Keewatin.

17: Madman Brown from Balmertown

A two-and-a-half hour drive north from the Trans-Canada Highway over a twisty, picturesque, two-lane road, past countless lakes and through endless forests, takes you to the area that in 1925 was the scene of a major gold rush. Some got rich, some moved on and some stayed, and the small neighboring communities of Red Lake, Madsen, Cochenour, Balmertown, and the tiny settlement on McKenzie Island, grew up clustering around the mine shafts. Their main economic underpinning is still the gold mining industry. Red Lake, on the shores of Howey Bay, is the main business centre. That is where the OPP located one of their detachments. Court was held — usually every two weeks — in the police building, and later in the adjacent Royal Canadian Legion.

There were many interesting people in and around Red Lake, and over the years I got to know most of them because of their court appearances or because they were in the flying business. In a way Madman Brown typified the rest of the community, in that you never knew what sort of an oddball character your client (or your opponent) was going to be. There were some real weirdos, many of whom would have been locked up in the funny farm had they been somewhere other than Red Lake, but Brown was the only one I was ever afraid of. Red Lake, of course, has always been one of my favorite places, partly because it produced so many strange characters. In the early days of my practice I had more paying clients in Red Lake than I did in Kenora, and even more importantly, they taught me a measure (perhaps not a big one) of humility. My Red Lake clients were the reason I never developed into a real tiger when I later became the Crown attorney.

Brown was somewhat of a joke around the courthouse and police office in Red Lake during the 1950s and early '60s. He suspected his wife of sleeping around, and he would beat her up regularly, or he would punch out her presumed lovers, thus landing him in court rather frequently. He was a big man, solid muscle with a mean disposition. To give you an idea of how strong he was, he worked at one of the local gold mines as a contract miner, but because of his disposition he could not keep a partner. He did the work of two men and took the bonus that normally would have been split by two men. One by one the Kenora lawyers defended him, but they refused to act for him a second time, and the day came when he had run through them all — all but me, for I had not yet become a Crown attorney.

I had just moved into my own office in Kenora. One Friday when I opened the mail there was a check for $100, and a note from Madman Brown saying that he would be in to see me Saturday afternoon to talk about a defense to his latest charge. I was concerned, because I knew all about his reputation for violence and would have preferred not to become involved. Later in the day I got a call from a friendly cop in Red Lake, it being before the time when cops and lawyers automatically considered themselves to be enemies. "Teddy," he said, "I hear you are going to be defending Brown. I hear he has really flipped out this time, and I want you to be careful. He apparently believes his old lady has been screwing Magistrate Fregeau and the inspector. His kid is too frightened to live at home and is staying with one of the local doctors." I knew from police office gossip that Mrs. Brown had moved out some time ago. His belief in Mrs. Brown's dalliance with the inspector and the magistrate was preposterous.

I didn't want to see Brown, but while I was pondering just how to get out of it gracefully I got a call from the old inspector, whom I held in considerable awe. "Lad," he said, "I'm coming over to see you at five o'clock. Now don't go home early." Click. I wondered what was coming.

The old inspector walked in promptly at five and sat down in what passed for my office. Furnishings were an ancient counsel table borrowed from the courthouse attic and a judge's chair that would suddenly throw the occupant out on the floor if he leaned back too far. Sheriff Bruce reserved these items for use by young lawyers who were having trouble getting an office together. Four plain wooden chairs purchased from Gork's Second Hand Store sat on a carpet my mother had taken out of storage where it had reposed for twenty years. To complete the antique look, I had a real fire going in the fireplace. I thought it much preferable to the glass and wood paneled boxes my colleagues had moved into back in southern Ontario, but I am not sure that it did anything to develop client confidence. Frankly, I didn't give a damn.

When the inspector walked in he pulled a beautiful little .32 Mauser automatic out of his pocket. "You probably know that I fired Constable

Adair the other day. I happen to know that he stiffed you for thirty-five dollars, which is about what this little gun is worth. I took the little gun from him and I am givin' it to you. Mind you use it right, and don't pull it on anyone unless you're willin' to shoot it. Corporal Bender at Red Lake tells me that son-of-a-bitch Brown is comin' to see you tomorrow, and it doesn't cost anything to be prepared." I was quite astonished at the speed with which news gets around.

With that the inspector showed me how to tape the gun to the desk by my right knee, where I could snatch it in a hurry. I kept the little gun for many years and I only ever had to pull it out twice. I never fired it in anger.

By the time Saturday afternoon rolled around I was petrified, having imagined all the dire things the demon Brown might do to me and my lovely office. I not only taped the gun to the desk leg, I brought my wife's German shepherd in and tied him to the hot air register. I told him to act real mean, which was quite unnecessary, because he was real mean by natural inclination; however, he chose this occasion to be out of character.

When Brown walked in and sat down the dog lunged so hard at his chain that he yanked the grille right off the wall. He bounded over to Brown and put his head in the villain's lap, inviting an ear scratching. Brown murmured and patted the dog and spoke to him like an old friend. Before I had even a small opportunity to tell Mr. Brown to take a hike, thereby incurring his wrath, he said in a perfectly normal voice, "Mr. Burton, I've thought it over and I am going to defend this one myself. Sorry to have troubled you."

I handed Mr. Brown his $100 retainer check and heaved a sigh of relief as he walked out the door. The dog actually looked sorry to see him go.

18: Hudson and Barilko, The Missing Flyers

1951 was a great year for adventures — other people's as well as my own. It was the year hockey idol Bill Barilko and his pal Dr. Henry Hudson went missing on a fishing trip to Hudson Bay, several hundred miles north of Timmins. I got to know all about it because I was working for Algoma Steel at the time, either in the bush prospecting or underground at the Helen Iron Mine in the little town of Wawa, perched up on the frigid north shore of Lake Superior.

It was a time when highgrading, or theft of gold, was a constant problem at all the mines. Thieving workers found ingenious ways of defying various security measures to smuggle out their pilfered bits and chunks of ore, and there was always a shady buyer to be found on the outside.

Barilko and Hudson were said to have the slickest little highgrading ring in all of Canada going for them at Timmins. Whatever happened in Timmins was immediately known in every mining town in Canada, even in mines that mined something other than gold. But it wasn't just the romantic link of thievery by well-known characters that drew public attention. To northern dwellers the fact that the two men might be down in the bush somewhere, injured or starving, was a strong point of interest.

As I recall it, the lunchroom rumors were to the effect that the rascals had packed a float compartment on each side of Doctor Hudson's aircraft full of semi-refined gold and were absconding to the Bahamas. The proponents of this theory ignored the fact that the little Fairchild airplane would not have been able to carry a bag of feathers with two adult passengers and gear on board. They also conveniently ignored the fact that it would be highly unlikely that a floatplane could fly down the eastern seaboard of the United States and across to the Bahamas without being noticed. But in my experience people who hold, or think they hold, the key to mysteries, are often not concerned with minor obstacles to their version of the truth. And I have to admit that this version of events fuelled at least a week of lunchroom chitchat, and was a welcome relief to the talk of whose wife was sleeping with whom while her husband was on shift. The theory of the flight to the Bahamas was exploded forever when it was learned that Hudson and Barilko had indeed been fishing at Hudson Bay, and the time of their departure from the Seal River was known.

I put the matter out of my mind until the fall of 1952, when I started my brilliant academic career at the University of Western Ontario, in London, Ontario, a bastion of conservatism, and the home of a number of insurance companies, including one for which my landlord worked. Landlord explained that whenever something unusual happened to an insured that had several policies with different companies, or perhaps to two people with multiple policies, one company would carry the ball for all of them, otherwise there would be investigators falling all over each other. Landlord's company held a policy on the life of one of the missing men, and on behalf of all was resisting efforts by the next of kin to collect on the policies. They did not want to pay, as they thought there was something to the theory of the escape to the Bahamas with the pot of gold.

Time marched on, and eventually I learned that the families of the two missing men did in fact collect on the policies, as a presumption of death had clicked in. This presumption becomes operative when a person has not been seen or heard of for a certain period of time. The route from the fishing camp on Hudson Bay to Timmins had been criss-crossed thousands of times by hundreds of airplanes and no trace of the little Fairchild had ever been seen. So the insurance companies paid, but not a minute before they had to.

Now, just a little digression here; this opportunity is too good to waste. Many years ago a very senior lawyer told me that if I ever got a chance to chastise an insurance company or a chartered bank I should do it, such being a moral obligation on a young lawyer. I did not have an opportunity to take a poke at an insurance company on this occasion, but I mention the matter to explain how my own disillusionment with insurance companies took root and flourished. It should have been obvious to the bastards at some early stage that Hudson and Barilko never got back to civilization, and they should have paid up on the legitimate policies to the families who needed the money, without quibbling.

In the course of time I became a lawyer and a Crown attorney, and quite friendly with the Precious Metals Theft Squad, later called the Anti-Highgrade Theft Squad, of the Ontario Provincial Police. I learned that the boys had indeed been in the highgrade business. The good doctor would buy highgrade gold from Timmins miners, beneficiate it somewhat — that is, hammer some of the host rock away — and then hand it off to the hockey player. He, in turn, would wrap the stuff in old smelly jock straps where it would remain undisturbed by US Customs when he crossed the border on hockey trips. To the uninitiated I will point out that there is absolutely nothing more vile than the jock strap of a hockey player, effectively discouraging any search by customs officials. Once in the States, Barilko would hand the gold off to a buyer and go on his way. The police knew about the activities of the two men (or so they said) and were about to pounce (or so they said) when they went missing.

In the summer of 1962 a commercial flight was scud running north from Cochrane to Moosonee when the pilot caught a flash of aluminum in a heavily wooded area. He did a tight turn, but could not locate the spot again. Being a quick thinker he threw several rolls of toilet paper over the side. His plan worked, as the forest was festooned with white, making it easy for a ground party to locate the downed aircraft. The bodies of Henry Hudson and Bill Barilko were identified from medical records eleven years after the crash of their little airplane.

During the intervening years it never occurred to me to inquire if there was any gold found in the Fairchild, until in 1999 I was in correspondence with George Crandall, (not his real name), a pal from the days when I so cheerfully prosecuted highgraders. I asked him about the gold, and he replied, “I was doing police work in the Timmins area when the plane was found. I’m told there wasn’t a speck of gold on board. You can bet that if I had been on the search there certainly wouldn’t have been any gold found, but I would have taken an early retirement.”

19: The Mad Magyar, Tony Karlich

The "Mad Magyar" moniker was hung on Tony Karlich when he arrived in the Kenora area in the late 1950s with a group of refugees, at the time of the Hungarian Revolution. He was not Hungarian, but it suited his purpose to be thought of as one, as he hoped people would forgive his wild and crazy carrying on if they thought he was a genuine Hungarian freedom fighter. I guess they did, too, for a while, but when his peccadilloes became serious everyone just wished he would go away. It soon became obvious that he was just hitching a ride on the coat tails of mostly kind and decent people who were trying to make a new life. If there had been a proper immigration screening procedure in place he would have been exposed as a thief and a fraud before he ever got to Canada. As it was, he set about following his old practices as soon as he set foot in the New World, and the police were after him again.

Karlich first came to my attention when I defended him on some petty charge — probably beating up on his girlfriend — and getting him acquitted by some stroke of benign fate, which he certainly did not deserve. For some reason he thought I was hot stuff, and he sought my assistance on several occasions after that. The Mad Magyar frequently beat hell out of Elizabeth Sinclair, and on one occasion he tried to pay me with money he had stolen from Elizabeth's mother. Not exactly what you'd call a nice guy. He finally got it through his head that I really did not want to act for him no matter how much money he was willing to pay me.

The general public wonders why the authorities don't simply put jerks like Karlich back on the next plane to wherever they came from, but it's not that easy. First of all, it may be difficult to prove precisely what was the land of the villain's origin, and that was the case with Karlich. We knew it wasn't Hungary, but which of several other misery-ridden places it might have been eluded the government of the day. Or so they said.

Second, the land of origin often simply won't accept them back, and that, too, could have been the case with The Mad Magyar, Magyar of course being what we thought was the Hungarian word for "Hungarian."

Finally, it is a fact that some eastern European countries executed returning deportees almost before they could say hello to their mothers, because of their prior misdeeds. The "League of Soft Hearted Do-Gooders" raised objections to Canadian involvement in such prisoner returns, resulting in inactivity on the part of our politicians, who turned to jelly when faced with the prospect of deporting criminals. Whatever the Communists were, they were certainly not soft on crime.

For all the above reasons Tony Karlich thought he had a pretty safe haven in Canada, and I suppose he had, too. For a livelihood he committed petty thefts and sponged off Elizabeth Sinclair's family on the McKenzie Portage Reserve. The people on the reserve were terrified of Tony and often refused to testify against him. When he needed fattening up he would do something to piss off Chief Russ O'Connor of the Keewatin Town Police; this usually netted him time in the district jail, where the grub was pretty good. O'Connor grew to detest the very thought of Karlich, and because of severe arthritic problems he did not relish the prospect of the inevitable foot chase.

One day in mid-winter after he had been out of jail long enough to cause O'Connor to build up a full head of resentment, Karlich did something serious enough to oblige O'Connor to give chase. The Mad Magyar found himself trapped, and to escape he jumped into the partly frozen Winnipeg River and commenced to drown. O'Connor ignored the pleas of the onlookers to the effect that he should let the bastard drown, and in spite of his failing health he managed to drag him ashore. Far from showing gratitude, Karlich picked up a sizeable rock and "beaned" O'Connor with it as he came up the bank. Bystanders pinned Karlich until O'Connor could recover and put cuffs on his prisoner. This time Karlich went to jail for a long time, but the federal authorities still would not deport him to his own country, which eventually turned out to be an eastern European nation.

Russ O'Connor, now retired and living on the cold north shore of Lake Superior in the village of Red Rock, recently reminded me of another Karlich escapade, and here is his verbatim account:

"We picked up Tony and his girlfriend on the McKenzie Portage Road for robbing an individual at Peterson's sawmill of around eighty dollars. They had a folding knife with about a six-inch blade that Tony called his *cheeken* knife, as he couldn't say chicken too well because of his accent. We later searched the area where the robbery happened and found the knife in the bush where he had thrown it.

Myself and another young constable brought them into the OPP detachment and searched Tony, with no luck. In the meantime the constable let the girlfriend go to the bathroom before we could get a matron to search her. Needless to say there was no money after that. It was around eleven in the evening and when we were trying to decide what to do next, Inspector T.G. Corsie came into the office. He decided to do some police work rather than give us shit. He got the Kenora works department superintendent to bring down the sewer maps for the courthouse area, got rubber boots and rakes, and sent everyone into the sewer, including himself, and then had all the toilets flushed and taps turned on. Before long the money came floating along and was retrieved to the last dollar. He then took off the boots, straightened his suit and went home with his rake and never mentioned it again. Tony and his girl were duly dealt with."

Holding forth in court.

At the time of this incident the OPP office was in the basement of the courthouse, and the inspector lived in a government house right next door. The sewer manholes were right in the middle of the street outside the courthouse.

Inevitably Karlich got out of jail again and happily (but stupidly) returned to his old ways. One of the several police forces in the area picked him up and drove him to be deposited in the district jail for safekeeping pending his trial. Passing by the frozen Lake of the Woods, he leaped from the cruiser, legging it out for Coney Island across the bay. The police chased him over the ice for a while, but gave it up when he swam across open water, climbing out on the other side and continuing his escape. The police drove around to a winter ice road that led to the south side of Coney Island, and were just in time to see Karlich run out onto the ice, heading in the direction of the McKenzie Portage Reserve. This route entailed another leap into an open portion of the lake and a swim to solid ice.

Knowing that Karlich would make for Elizabeth Sinclair's house, the police drove back around through Kenora, past Keewatin, positioning themselves at Sinclair's door. Poor old Karlich was all in when they tucked him into the back seat of the cruiser after first removing a twelve-inch bayonet from under his coat. No one was very sorry for him, not even his beloved Elizabeth.

This time the authorities took the action they should have taken long ago. They decided that since he came from a Hungarian jail (as many genuine Hungarian Freedom Fighters had) he belonged back there, whether the Hungarians liked it or not. So back he went. Magistrate Fregeau made inquiries of Interpol and was told that once Karlich set foot on home soil, a firing squad was convened to deal with him for the greater good of society. I never heard how the do-gooders reacted to the information, but I can attest that all the law enforcement agencies around the Kenora area were gratified by the news.

20: Minaki

I debated leaving this chapter out, because leaving it in could have such a negative effect on the reader. However, earlier in the book I undertook to tell truth, and this grubby stuff is all part of the truth. In mitigation I want the reader to know that there were many fine people in Minaki and at the Whitedog Reserve a few miles further north, and they more than make up for the depraved (and deprived) people who populate the next few pages of this book.

When I was called to the bar of the Province of Ontario in 1959 I immediately returned to Kenora and set up a practice. A lot of action for a young lawyer aspiring to do criminal law came out of Minaki, but there wasn't enough money in it to support a pet gerbil. In spite of the lack of money, I accepted the work, and it didn't take me long to get to know the people. I was helped considerably by a series of police officers that had not succumbed to the view that defense lawyers were "The Enemy."

Minaki was a little village of 300 or so up on the north line of the Canadian National Railway. Nearby, the shore and islands of the Winnipeg River were home to a number of secluded cottages of varying degrees of opulence, populated during the summer months by families, mostly from Winnipeg, arriving by train. The excuse for the village's existence was a beautiful resort on the edge of town, built many years previously to attract people to travel on the CNR. The marvelous lodge of quarried stone and pine logs was not financially stable and eventually closed in the 1970s, even though the Province of Ontario had injected a number of millions of dollars into improvements. Its demise wasn't much of a blow to the community, as the lodge had employed very few Minaki or Whitedog people. Subsequent owners all successively lost money on the lodge and it ended up on the hands of the Province, which eventually transferred it to the Whitedog Band of Indians. For years it sat forlornly, like an abandoned bride, on the shore of the wild and beautiful Winnipeg River. There no longer were Saturday dances in the ballroom or shouts of joy from the golf course, tennis courts and swimming pools. The ski hill and the landing strip became overgrown by bush. They tell me that the lodge and many of the surrounding guest quarters were vandalized and the furnishings stolen, and it became as desolate as the village itself.

In the late 1960s they finally punched a road through to Minaki from Highway 17. Until then you could reach it by rail from east or west, by boat on the Winnipeg River from Kenora, or by floatplane. Some of the residents had lived all their lives in Minaki without ever seeing the "outside."

It was in Minaki that the phenomenon of track suicides first reared its ugly head. Track deaths were common beginning in the '60s, but they were attributed to accidents. The prevailing opinion was that it simply wasn't in the culture of Indians to commit suicide. (Note that I am using the term "Indian" because at this point the term "First Nations" was not in use.) However at some point a coroner's inquest dropped notions of political correctness and called a track death a suicide. It was not until then that the outside world began to realize just how dreadfully unhappy the Indian people of the North had become. Once the fact of suicides was recognized as such, it seemed to speed up the frequency of track deaths. The homicide rate in the area also seemed to accelerate, although I admit to speaking anecdotally and not from hard statistics. Occasionally it became difficult to determine whether a death was a suicide or a homicide. Such was the case of the high rock beside the tracks that became known as "Lorne Martin's Leap" or was it "(name deleted)'s Push."

One of the more rotten jokes about Minaki was: "What sound does the train make going through Minaki?" Answer: "Clickety-click…clickety-click…clickety-click…clickety-click…clickety-squish…clickety-squish." Now, you may think that is revolting and insensitive, but my observation is that is the way people begin to think when they are exposed to blood and guts and death over a period of time. It is a sort of compensating mechanism that prevents them from becoming hardened to the extent that they simply accept that the blood and gore is a normal state of affairs. Police, fire fighters and military people will know what I am talking about.

There was no such thing as a typical crime in Minaki and environs. Each one was revolting in some new way. Each new murder was an exercise in horror. Violent death became commonplace.

Mary Jane Oshie was only a little bitty thing, maybe ninety pounds and five feet tall. She was well known in all the government systems in Kenora — courts, police, welfare, Children's Aid, hospital, and so on. Her chief problem was her displaced hip, common among the Ojibway, which made it difficult to run away fast enough from people who wanted

Minaki Lodge in the 1950s: an oasis of luxury in the northern Ontario bush.

to beat her up, people like Dennis Kelly. She had a weakness for booze, too. But she never stole anything or hurt anyone.

She didn't deserve to die that way, with a cold steel crow bar shoved up her private parts. She lived with her boyfriend, Dennis Kelly, in a squalid semi-permanent bush camp at Cygnet Lake, near Minaki, along with a number of Dennis' brothers, hangers-on, boyfriends, and female companions. I won't say husbands and wives, because marriage was not a status one would concede to the relationships that only flourished briefly, then degenerated into acrimonious bickering and assaults. Between them the men cut enough wood to pay for a few groceries and rotgut wine, always wine. The Children's Aid Society took many of the babies as soon as they were born. Even so there were several older children left pathetic, hungry ragamuffins.

I want to digress to give you another vignette, something that had happened in another trial years before. We had all — counsel, judge and other witnesses — been calling a female Indian witness by her first name. There was no disrespect intended, it was just what you did in those days. My father was sitting in the courtroom as an observer, taking it all in. When it was time for the morning coffee break the old judge invited defense counsel, myself, the sheriff, and Pop into his office. The old gentleman asked Pop, as a layperson and a member of the public, what he thought of the proceedings.

Pop scratched his chin for a moment before replying. "My Lord, I am very favorably impressed with the quality of the justice I see in this courtroom. The accused is certainly getting a fair trial, no doubt about it. But I feel bound to tell you that in one small way there is a chink in the dignity of the court."

The judge leaned forward, the better to confront whatever it was that Pop had to say.

Pop went on. "Throughout the whole morning no one has ever referred to Ida as anything other than Ida. She is married to Ivan Petawanaquib and is his wife in every respect, just as much as our wives are our lawfully wedded wives. She may or may not have been married in a church, but no one has troubled to ask her. Even if she was not married in a church, she is that man's wife by custom and tradition and deserves the same respect that our wives do. When referring to her or addressing her by name in English she should be called Mrs. Petawanaquib, not Ida."

I halfway expected the judge to explode, but he did not. He nodded his head gravely, saying, "Quite right, Mr. Burton, quite right. Gentlemen, that's the way we will do it from here on."

One does not hear Indian women automatically called by their first names now.

The reason for the digression was simply to emphasize that respect and disrespect can be shown in many small ways, one of the subtler being to refrain from giving people a title of some sort. I hope my lack of respect for the people at the Cygnet Lake camp is plain. Under just about any other circumstances I would have referred to them as husbands and wives.

But on with the story of the unhappy demise of Mary Jane Oshie, also known as "Step-And-A-Half."

One Saturday in the late 1970s the clan headed into Kenora, probably by taxi, to buy groceries and booze, and to have a few drinks in a bar. Dennis Kelly and Mary Jane Oshie had no money, but they did have a couple of bottles of wine left over from the last trip to town. They remained behind in camp, commencing to drink their wine as soon as the taxi was out of sight. There were no independent witnesses left to say what happened while they were alone.

When the gang returned they were pretty well hammered out of shape, except for one kid who was still too young to share any more booze than she could swipe from her elders. She told about the scene that confronted them when they walked into camp. Mary Jane was lying on a bed, dying, groaning her last. The adults in the room ignored her. She then appeared to merely pass out, not an unusual state of affairs at Cygnet Lake, until someone noticed the large quantity of blood pooling under the bed. Further investigation revealed that Step-And-A-Half was bleeding from between her legs. There was no apparent external cause of the bleeding. Dennis professed to know nothing about Mary Jane's death. No stick or other weapon that could have caused injury was found either by the quickly sobered family group or by the police from Minaki. But since Dennis had exclusive opportunity, he was charged with Mary Jane's murder. It was a dreadfully weak charge until the offending weapon showed up, but even then we had no motive. Juries always like to see a motive even though it is not an absolute necessity in law.

At some stage during the closing phase of the investigation the child who had remained sober handed Constable Woody Linton a bloody iron crowbar. Woody had not actually seen where the child found the crowbar, making it necessary to put the child on the stand at trial to say for herself where she found it. Blood was identified on the bar, and even though the Center of Forensic Science can do marvels, they could not say for sure that it was human blood, much less that it was Mary Jane's blood. At the preliminary hearing we had skated by this point without going into a lot of detail, and I tried to do the same at trial. But the cross examination by defense counsel was to come. Ah, the purifying crucible of cross-examination! Or so the legal textbooks call it. But they fail to give equal billing to the warning that counsel should never ask a question to which he does not know the answer.

The questioning went like this:

Q: You say you found the bar behind the house?
A: Yes.
Q: Where behind the house?
A: Beside the woodpile.
Q: How did you happen to notice the bar beside the woodpile?
A: I seen a dog licking it.
Q: Why would a dog be licking a crowbar?
A: Because there was blood on it. That man used it to kill Mary Jane.

Bingo, I knew we had Dennis by the short hairs! Even though we never did show a motive I knew the jury would balance the lack against the dramatic and unexpected evidence of the child. The jury did indeed forgive the Crown for the lack of evidence of motive. They convicted Dennis Kelly and he went away for a long time.

It was a perfect example of asking one question too many, a trap the legal texts warn law students about.

You can imagine the effect the child's testimony had on the jury. They practically fell over themselves in their efforts to get to the jury room and find Dennis guilty, even though the Crown was quite unable to show any motive for the killing. There was no confession and there were no eyewitnesses. The little girl's very articulate and highly appropriate answer was a complete surprise to everyone, including Constable Linton and me.

Woody Linton, one of only two Minaki police officers at the time, got credit for a brilliant investigation. To this day he shamelessly accepts that credit.

As a postscript, I will say that Dennis' father, Albert, an equally scruffy and disreputable character, walked into my office shortly after the jury brought in the verdict of guilty, and jumped on Woody's back. Woody applied a judo hold and flipped him onto the floor, hard, much to the delight of my secretary, Lucy. Albert left him alone after that. On another occasion several of Dennis' brothers cornered Woody in the bush and advanced on him with the obvious intention of committing mayhem. This time Woody very wisely did not tangle with them, but took to his heels. I have to say that the reaction shown by the Kelly family was most unusual, as most Aboriginal people were appreciative of a fair trial. Over the years I was treated to far more compliments than threats by accused persons and their families. The few threats that came my way were neutralized by more serious counter threats.

Malachi was another Minaki satellite with more than its share of lawlessness. One night in the wee hours Woody received a hurry-up call to go to Malachi to look into an unusual death. Catching the next freight train, he and a visiting constable rode through the night to Malachi. Pounding on the door of the general store they learned that the newly departed was lying in state in a shack on the other side of the lake. They commandeered a boat, making their way across the black water to a cluster of shacks that belonged to a notoriously troublesome and dangerous clan of local people who wanted the police the hell out of there. An old-fashioned wake was in progress, complete with vile home brew, store-bought whiskey and wine, and ancestral chanting. Some of the ancestors were Irish and some were Ojibway, which did not do anything to create a peaceful atmosphere.

Woody merely wanted to preserve the body until a coroner could relay his instructions via the phone at the general store by the tracks across the lake. The situation heated up to nearly the flash point.

Woody's companion was quick to size the situation up. Legging it down the trail to the boat he shouted over his shoulder, "I'm going to go after help. You stay here and guard the body."

Woody was in a dangerous predicament, with a dozen or so liquored up men and women all vying for the privilege of taking him out, and the nearest phone being across the lake and quite inaccessible. Nevertheless he stuck with it until dawn, when a Beaver aircraft from Kenora appeared with a couple of well-armed police officers to take over from Woody.

I don't know whatever happened to Woody's constable companion who ducked out when the going got rough, and perhaps it is just as well. Woody, however, has become a legend in Northwestern Ontario, and the other guy has not.

I did not set out to write a full-fledged sociological treatise about Minaki and environs, but perhaps you can stand one more story, this time about Whitedog, some thirty-five miles downstream from Minaki on the Winnipeg River. Guy Hunter was not one of the better-respected people on the Whitedog Reserve because he periodically used to beat the bejesus out of his wife. Other men at Whitedog did the same thing, but Guy had the reputation of being more vigorous about it. One day in the late 1970s he overdid it, and sent her into the next world. Or perhaps he shot her. It doesn't really matter, sadly.

Disposing of the body created a problem. Guy had heard all about bodies in the water coming to the surface, and he was afraid his wife would be found if he just jettisoned her on an island. He vacillated for four hot days in the summer, trying (unsuccessfully, as it turned out) to keep his grisly cargo out of sight. Eventually the body bloated up to four times its normal size and could be smelled for a mile over calm water. The lady was in the shape of a huge amorphous triangle when the police found her jammed into the pointed bow of a fishing boat.

Now the police had a problem in deciding what to do with the body. Moving it to the morgue in Kenora was out of the question, so they flew the pathologist up to the place on the Winnipeg River where the boat and its passenger were tied up. Dr. Pan was equal to the occasion. Taking only a scalpel and a retractor, he stepped into the water and attempted to do a post mortem examination on the body by standing next to the boat on the upwind side. The boat, however, was too unsteady. Dr. Pan untied the boat and pushed it over to the float of the Beaver, intending to tip the body out onto the float where he could more readily perform his examination.

The body was not amenable. The stalwarts assisting Dr. Pan all heaved together, but instead of staying on the float the body simply rolled off the other side into the Winnipeg River. When they attempted to grasp the body, pieces of it came away in their hands. The situation was becoming serious, as the police feared valuable evidence might be lost. They finally solved the problem by working a piece of canvas under the body to form a large sling, tying it to the float of the aircraft, and flying it to Kenora.

These anecdotes give you something of the ambiance of Minaki. But it was a good place to visit if you weren't a police officer or a social worker. Once the road made it accessible, Erica and I loved to go to the Saturday night dances. We alternated between the country dances in the schoolhouse, where the local gents showed up in bush boots, the food was cheese and crackers and you drank beer out of the bottle, and the dances at the Minaki Lodge ballroom with a professional dance band brought in from Winnipeg, formal dress, fine wines, and caviar to go with the crackers.

Minaki was a place of extremes, and I guess it still is. Twelve police officers and an army of social workers are trying to change it. One hopes they will be successful.

Today the little village of Minaki remains much the same. Cottages and tourist lodges have proliferated in the area as more and more people have come to appreciate the beauty of the lake and river system and the vast expanse of wilderness. In recent years, new owners have taken possession of Minaki Lodge, and it holds promise of rising to its former glory and becoming again, as it once was called, the Jewel of the North.

Note: In 2003, the grand log building burned to the ground in a spectacular conflagration that could be seen for miles. Speculation was rampant, but the cause was never determined.

21: The Children's Aid Society Goes North

The two main complaints about children's aid societies in the North are that, (1) they take too many children into care and, (2) they don't take enough children into care. Well-intentioned social workers feel they are in a no-win situation. As far as I can tell this situation still prevails, even though most reserves have banded together with other reserves to form their own child service agencies.

I was on the board of the Kenora Children's Aid Society back in the 1960s and, either in that capacity or as Crown attorney, I was constantly on the receiving end of such complaints. Feeling, as I did, that the CAS workers had an almost impossible task, I tended to give the complainers pretty short shrift. Not always, mind you, as some dreadful things happened, such as the young male social worker who took a fifteen-year-old girl to bed with him and swore up and down that it was only so he could hypnotize her into a virtuous state of mind.

But this story is about something good that was done by two untrained but well motivated social workers with big hearts and a lot of common sense. I am aware that much that has been recounted so far has been about people who aren't very smart, or very nice, and I don't want you to think that I am preoccupied solely with that type of person.

As a board member with a hands-on approach I was appointed to the personnel committee, and I got to know the field workers well. Episodes of a worker fleeing down the tracks on a handcar with a baby in his arms were not commonplace, but nor were they unknown. We paid our workers well by the standards of the industry, and were able to hire a director for $10,000 a year, a princely sum. Motivation, rather than paper qualifications, is what we looked for. The "culture" of the Kenora CAS was such that the social workers knew they would be backed up if they did something new, or different. This is where Jack Copeland and Peter Louttit came into the picture.

When we hired him in the early 1960s, Peter Louttit was in his thirties, an ex-Airforce pilot, and had been a children's aid kid himself. As a bonus he was Cree, and had some understanding of the problems of the Native people. At the time we hired him he was flying a Cessna 180 and a Norseman for Parsons Airways. Peter had no educational qualifications to be a social worker, but the board of directors (except for the "blue-rinse" ladies) was darn glad to have him.

Jack Copeland was another social worker the like of which could not be found attached to any CAS other than Kenora. He was a free trader in the Whitedog area on the Winnipeg River, which flows northerly out of Lake of the Woods, and was pushing sixty years of age when we hired him. He ran a small sawmill on the side, which meant sporadic jobs for five or six men from the reserve, but it was not very profitable to Jack. He and Mrs. Copeland wanted to spend their declining years in town rather than in the bush and, as a speaker of the Ojibway language, Jack was a natural for the CAS. Charlie Wingfield, the other member of the personnel committee, and I, had to push a little to get him by the blue-rinse ladies and the officials in the Ministry of Social Services, but in the end everyone was quite pleased with him.

Louttit and Copeland were well aware of the difficulty of placing Native children for adoption. Placing them in Kenora soon ceased to be an option, as there was a shortage of adoption homes, and the troubles and misery that abounded on the nearby reserves made them undesirable locations for the numerous children that passed through the hands of the society. Placing children through other children's aid societies in other parts of the province, most often in white homes, did not seem proper to Louttit and Copeland. Even though there was as yet no demand for it from First Nations people, they decided something different had to be done.

In the winter of 1975, or thereabouts, Peter leased a Cessna 185 from his former employer and headed into the far north with Jack Copeland. They took with them the files of several Native children awaiting adoption, and stopped down at a number of villages that had never had a visit from a social worker of any kind. We now hear a lot about self-government, but we don't hear that until quite recently "Native custom" adoptions worked quite well, at least in the far north where such practices were carried on without interference from the bureaucracy.

When the men returned two weeks later they had completed a number of home studies and taken applications for adoptions from good homes in several villages. These homes did not have running water, and probably no electricity, but they contained a lot of love. Unconditional love for children is one of the finer characteristics of the Indian race, and the homes where this was strongest were the ones chosen by Louttit and Copeland. They were prepared to convince the District Judge that they had used good judgment in their proposed placements. They had meticulously documented their cases, right down to photographs of the toothbrushes lined up at the washbasins by the wood stoves that were a feature of most northern homes. They devised a scheme that was an acceptable marriage of Native custom and the law of the land, for which read "white man's law." District Judge G.F. Kinsman approved.

A few weeks later Copeland and Louttit took off from the late winter ice and flew north again. This time ten children ranging from babes-in-arms to a twelve-year old accompanied them. They took the much larger Norseman, a fabric-covered, smoke-belching monster that had helped open up the north in its time. Now obsolete, but very, very serviceable, it was the last chariot one might imagine to be the carrier of a group of children heading for a new life. It was said that the interior of the Norseman was so festooned with diapers and blankets that it looked like an advertisement for a layette sale.

Two weeks later the old gray Norseman sat down in the slush on the spring ice back in Kenora, throwing up twin clouds of water from the skis. Ten children had been placed in villages all the way from Sandy Lake to Hudson Bay. The exercise of finding adoptive homes in this manner was a first, and could not have happened except among people who value children greatly.

As of 2002, most bands have joined together with other bands to form their own family service organizations. In my view this is a good start on self-government. One hopes they will develop concepts of justice more in keeping with the Charter of Rights, which will be the real test of the ability of First Nations people to be self governing.

22: The McKenzie Island Bank Robbery

He had half a dozen nicknames — Cool Hand Hans, The Great McKenzie Island Bank Robber, and so on — none of them very flattering. No one was very sorry to see this pathetic figure of fun, for whom no one could even think of an appropriate nickname, deported back to wherever he came from when the government of the day (Conservative I believe) finally summoned up the courage to send him back to his place of origin.

Hans Handke had found his way over to Canada after the war and, in spite of his disabilities, the chief of which was his monumental stupidity, he managed to land a high-paying job in one of the mines at Red Lake. The year was about 1962.

As was the fashion among Red Lake miners at the time, he took to wife, or at least to bed, a lassie from one of the northern reserves, one Ann Marie Redsky, who was pure in neither mind nor body. As I understood it, the arrangement was that Ann Marie was to provide Hans with all the nookie he could handle and he was to supply the room and board. And the wine, of course. And he was not to get too upset if she acquired other boyfriends temporarily. Hans was more dismayed to find that Ann Marie's whole family came with her than he was about the boyfriends, as he had to feed the family, although what they did for him is not recorded. That is just as well, as I am hoping this book will be considered suitable for family reading.

In due course Hans ran out of money, what with all those extra mouths to feed, so he decided to rob a bank. Choosing the Bank of Nova Scotia on McKenzie Island as his target was his first act of colossal stupidity because he had to walk back and forth over the ice road to the mainland, and many people recognized him from shore or from passing vehicles. The moccasin telegraph being what it is, everyone in McKenzie Island, Cochenour, Balmertown, Madsen and Red Lake very soon knew all about the bank robbery, who did it, and where he was, from moment to moment.

A further act of monumental stupidity was in donning an ill-fitting scarf that disguised his features, but did nothing to disguise his voice. A final act of stupidity was in the temporary stashing of the loot in a trash barrel in full view of everyone, out in front of Fergie's General Store. The good people of McKenzie Island were not going to see THEIR bank robbed by anyone, particularly not some jerk from the mainland, and they were quick to notify Fergie that his trash barrel contained something more than empty cigarette packages.

Now, a wee digression here, if you please. I have always been fascinated by signs, be they fortunetellers' signs, Burma Shave signs, or the sign on Fergie's general store. It looked something like this:

GENERAL
Fergies
STORE

The hand lettering was pretty crude, but I am sure you get the idea.

When the police from Red Lake got to General Fergie's trash barrel they found that Fergie had wrapped the money up in a paper bag and was just waiting for them. McKenzie Island people are well known to be the salt of the earth but were not altogether free from earthly temptations as the accounts receivable side of Fergie's ledger would have shown, and it was generally conceded that Fergie had done the right thing in seizing and wrapping the boodle.

As it happened the robbery took place on the day Magistrate's Court was in session over on the mainland. It was but the work of a few moments to swear an information, whisk poor old Hans before the court, accept his heartfelt plea of guilty and send him on his way. It was probably before the days of Legal Aid.

You may think those were enough acts of immense stupidity for one man, but I have to tell you that there was one more. Hans may have been stupid, but he was persistent. He pined for his ladylove, the beautiful Ann Marie, and tried several times to break out of the Stoney Mountain Penitentiary, but without success. Stoney Mountain in Manitoba was where they sent the really bad boys from that part of the country at that time, as opposed to district jails. Hans eventually hit upon an admirable strategy, and it would have worked if it had not been for a nosy postal clerk.

Hans Handke has the distinction of being the only person to escape from the pen by mailing himself out. Well, nearly out. Hans managed to secrete himself in one of Her Majesty's mailbags just before it was thrown on the truck. An alert postal clerk noticed there were large moving lumps in the bag, and knowing there were no raccoons within the walls at Stoney Mountain he decided a closer investigation would be in order. Imagine his surprise when Hans popped out of the bag! An extra two years was tacked on to his sentence, but as things turned out he didn't have to serve it.

The result of the Great McKenzie Island Bank Fiasco was that Hans was deported to his homeland, leaving Ann Marie to grieve for what might have been.

The bank robbery and Hans' undying love for Ann Marie were not the only things we remember McKenzie Island for. McKenzie Island was home to the Gold Eagle Hotel, the most civilized watering hole in Northern Ontario. I know, because I have hit them all in fifty years of roaming around the North in one capacity or another. In its latter years the hotel was run by retired bush pilot and all-round good guy Jimmy Cousineau, who insisted that everyone had a right to drink unmolested in his pub, even bush pilots, Crown attorneys and off-duty policemen. It was a sad day when the hotel burned down.

The Gold Eagle may be gone, but in The Snake Pit over in the Red Lake Inn they still talk about the day Hans Handke robbed the bank on McKenzie Island.

23: Anthony Jack

In the thirty-five years that I practiced law, I prosecuted or defended a great variety of cases. I have recounted some of the more interesting ones in a previous book, *Journal of a Country Lawyer: Crime, Sin and Damn Good Fun*. The case histories of a few court cases are included in this volume to entertain the reader with something other than my own personal adventures and misadventures. Of homicide cases alone, I had prosecuted well over fifty when I stopped counting. The story of Anthony Jack is just one of them.

Anthony Jack said he didn't really mean to shoot his friend Eli Oshie in the head, and that must have been enough to cast a reasonable doubt on the issue, as the jury acquitted him of capital murder and convicted him on the lesser charge of manslaughter. Anthony and Eli were both residents of a reserve close to Kenora and lived narrow little lives characterized by boredom. They fantasized a lot, always about shooting people and hurting them. They delighted in telling others about their fantasies. Anthony was pretty slow on the uptake and was forever blabbing about how it would feel to shoot someone in the head. His chance came sooner than he expected.

One pitch-black night in midsummer Anthony was picking his way down the gravel road that led to his house on the Whitefish Bay Reserve, adjacent to the village of Sioux Narrows, when he bumped into a taxi parked by the side of the road. He could tell by the voices that the occupants were the taxi driver and his friend Eli Oshie. They were engaged in a serious discussion on how it felt to die. Anthony quietly slipped into the car and almost immediately out again. He was put out that Eli and the taxi driver seemed to take no notice of him, and he simmered as he walked down the path to his parents' home. They took no notice of him either, which may be why Anthony was so mad at the world.

Anthony reached under his ramshackle bed and pulled out a thoroughly scratched and scarred .22-caliber Cooey rifle, the type of gun that has probably killed more people than any other gun in common usage in the North. Close inspection would have revealed it to be a piece of junk that would only fire if the bolt were held very firmly in place as the trigger was pulled. Anthony didn't really care, as he was only going to have to use it once.

Once again the other two men in the taxi did not seem to notice Anthony as he returned to the car, carrying on their discussion as if he was not there. Once again Anthony felt his cheeks burning. He slid a cartridge into the breech of the old rifle. As he pulled the bolt back to cock it he was very careful to hold it down with his thumb so the firing pin would operate properly. He gently put the muzzle to the back of Eli Oshie's head and pulled the trigger. Anthony Jack was surprised at the loudness of the report. He had expected a soft plop, but what he got was a plop followed by a sort of splash. He said later that it was only by a strong effort of will that he was not violently ill.

The taxi driver jumped out and hit the ground running, heading for the nearest telephone. He was so shaken up that he had trouble telling the operator what he wanted, it being the days before the dial exchange was installed for Sioux Narrows and Whitefish Bay. He was so incoherent that Anthony had a few extra minutes to make his escape.

Police in Kenora, Sioux Narrows and Nestor Falls were made aware of what had happened. All roads in the area were blocked, but somehow Anthony managed to squeeze by the police unobserved. Eventually he found a car with keys in it, out on the highway, so he headed south at top speed. Speeding was a mistake, as Anthony did not know how to drive at all, much less at high speed.

Anthony raced through Nestor Falls with the pedal to the floor, attracting a lot of attention with his roaring engine and screeching tires. Just south of Nestor Falls he lost all control, going through the right ditch and smashing into a grove of alders. When the police got to the scene, the tires of the stolen car were still smoking.

Ken Wilson was a newly appointed detective sergeant, and he was anxious to finish the case up as neatly as possible. He was whisked to the scene in a fast cruiser, arriving less than an hour after Anthony took to the bush in his stolen car. Taking charge immediately, Ken noted that the highway ran straight as a die through a large swampy area, but no one had seen Anthony on the road. Ken figured that Anthony was in the alders, probably not far from where he left the road. As a long-time bushman, he knew that Anthony would not get far through the alders in the dark.

No one knew what kind of a gun Anthony was carrying, or how good he was with it. Discretion being the better part of valor, Ken decided to call all the men out of the bush, taking all the risk himself. The going was tough, really tough. Ken had no light except an ordinary police issue flashlight, no searchlights or spotlights, but he strongly doubted that Anthony Jack would have any light at all. Fortunately he was right.

Just fifty yards off the roadway, and directly in line with the car, Ken was able to pick out an extra thick clump of bush by the feeble beam of his flashlight. Could it be that Anthony had made no further progress than this since going off the road? He clicked off his flashlight in order not to make a target in the dark.

"Come out of there you son-of-a-bitch or I'll blow your head off," shouted Ken, fingering his revolver with distaste, "and leave your gun where it is."

Ken need not have been concerned about the gun, as it was back on the Whitefish Bay Reserve in the back seat of the taxi. Anthony Jack was only too glad to stumble through the alders to open ground. He put out his hands to accept the cuffs without being told.

The case was only my second big one, and I thought I might get a conviction for capital murder out of it. I prepared it well, and presented it reasonably well, for a greenhorn. I wanted to convince the jury that if Anthony had to go to all that trouble to fire the gun with the sticking bolt, the act must have been pre-meditated, planned, and deliberate, but the jury apparently didn't see it my way, and convicted on the lesser, but included, offence of manslaughter. It wasn't the last time in my career that a jury disagreed with me.

Anthony Jack turned out to be a really bad dude, getting into more trouble down at Kingston Penitentiary. I don't know if he was ever paroled or served out his twenty years, but I am quite sure they never made him welcome back at Whitefish Bay.

24: Death of the Crow

The Rotinski family was not one of the better families in Dryden. John was a hulking brute who was always in the dock for some offence involving his fists, very often against his long-time lady friend, whom I remember only as Evelyn. They were a remarkably unattractive pair, and I can't understand what they saw in each other. Evelyn wanted John to marry her, but he would have none of it. They squabbled incessantly in their squalid home.

John's brother Andrew, known to all as "The Crow," lived with them. He was somewhat deformed, being stunted in his growth, with long arms and legs and a small torso, giving rise to his nickname. The Crow was a real pain in the neck to Evelyn and was a source of much of the contention in the home. Evelyn despised him, and even brother John didn't have much time for him, but it was nice to have the extra welfare money. (Incidentally, as far as I know The Crow was the only person ever charged with and convicted of impaired driving on a bicycle.)

On one bitterly cold winter evening in 1979 or so, John or Evelyn told Andrew to go out and get an armful of wood for the stove. All three had been drinking cheap wine, and no doubt they weren't being very polite to each other, or so Evelyn said in her statement to the police. It is important to note that this statement was deliberately taken before Evelyn sobered up and had the time or the wit to concoct lies about the events of the evening.

But to continue, Andrew sassed his older brother and refused to get the wood. Evelyn said John slapped Andrew, and then dragged him out to the porch by the scruff of his neck. John came in with some wood, but left Andrew out in the cold. Evelyn was too drunk to take any part in the affair.

In the morning Evelyn stepped out on the porch for firewood, and there was poor old Andrew, frozen stiff as a board. Naturally the Dryden Town Police were on the scene within minutes. They immediately perceived that the appropriate charge would be against John Rotinski, for criminal negligence causing death, which is really a species of manslaughter. They also perceived that the only way they could ever support a criminal charge would be on the evidence of Evelyn. Having had previous experience of Evelyn they knew she would recant anything damaging she said about John Rotinski once she sobered up. They called me early in the morning, before I was up, and I told them to take the statement anyway. We now had an ace in the hole, one with which we could impeach Evelyn later, if necessary. That statement was not in itself evidence against John, but could be used to impeach Evelyn if she said something different on the witness stand. That is the way the law stood at the time.

Clever, wasn't I?

But the bitch outfoxed me. She was all sweetness and light at the preliminary hearing, and she told her story just as I have recounted it here. But at trial she produced a paper certifying that just two days earlier she had lawfully wed one John Rotinski. As everyone knows, you can't require spouses to testify against each other.

Case closed.

And I thought this sort of thing happened only in cheap novels.

25: His Lordship the Weeper

That sounds like the moniker that might have attached to a Chicago underworld character during the 1930s, does it not? But I assure you that it belonged to a real live Ontario High Court judge during the 1960s or perhaps the '70s, and it attached for very good reason. His Lordship was a fine gentleman and a very good judge, but he cried crocodile tears when he had to perform the hard duty of sentencing young people to heavy time. On one occasion when he was sitting in Kenora he went out and personally purchased a number of boxes of Kleenex which he distributed to his clerk, to counsel, the two young rats who had shot and killed an old man for a few bucks, and anyone else within reach of the dais. He wept as he lectured them. He was so sincere that he caused all the onlookers to weep, too, all except the two young rats. I was told that he often carried on like that.

But if you think that is bizarre let me tell you what happened the night before the sentencing.

I was working late in my office, preparing the next case that was to come before the court. I was alone in the courthouse, even the cleaners having left, when the telephone rang. Larry the Weeper had seen me through the window, and returned to his hotel to call me to ask me to open the door. It didn't occur to me at the time that it was me he wanted to talk to, or I may have found some excuse to put him off. But how do you put off a High Court judge who merely wants you to open a door?

To my surprise His Lordship did not go down the hall to his own office, but followed me into mine.

"Mr. Burton, would you mind turning out the lights so we can't be seen from the street? You know some people might think it highly improper to be talking to you in the absence of opposing counsel."

"Damn right they would, and they would be right, too," I thought to myself. But you don't talk to High Court judges that way, at least not until you have a hell of a lot more seniority than I had. I decided to let it ride and see what developed.

"It seems obvious to me that these young men have never had the advantage of a proper upbringing. Their parents are not even present in the court room to give them support."

I told him neither of the boys knew who their fathers were, and it was likely that their mothers did not know either.

With that he started to cry real tears. Out came the Kleenex. I declined his offer of a blow. Perhaps he thought I was hard-hearted. In any event he redoubled his efforts to soften my heart. He wanted me to abandon the first-degree murder charge in favor of second-degree murder or even manslaughter, which would very plainly have been a cop-out, wrong in law and wrong by the prevailing standards of morality. There was no justification for such an act, other than mercy. Actually, mercy is probably not a bad reason for doing something like that, and later in my career I would not have had such a hard time with the judge's request. In due time I came to realize that even hard-nosed cops would not have disagreed with a decision to minimize the impact of the law on the two young fellows who were raised in such deprived circumstances, although I don't recall getting any pats on the back at the time.

The upshot was that on the following morning we went into court, and with mixed feelings I did my thing, advising the court that I was not asking the jury for a conviction on first-degree murder, but only on second-degree. Kleenex was handed around, and The Weeper went into a two-hour tirade. One of the boys was sentenced to seven years, and the other to five years. Neither had shed a tear, but the judge had, and he went up in my esteem for it.

26: Crime and the Tube

The closest most people get to crime, really low-down, sordid, offensive wrongdoing, is when they turn on their TV sets. Crime and violence then become entertainment, as very often we don't distinguish between the reality of the news and the fantasy of the police flicks. We may tell ourselves that our society is mature and not influenced by what we see on the tube, but that is wishful thinking. If we are not influenced by exposure to crime, either real or fanciful, then we must have become hardened or inured to it, and that in itself is a negative consequence of television. A case can be made that the whole of North American society is becoming increasingly callous to crime, shutting its mind to the more negative aspects of it, if not outright condoning it. To many individuals the personal consequences of focusing on TV crime are even more serious, although I am bound to observe that the vast majority of people are better able to make a distinction between sin, included in which is the concept of crime, on the one hand, and fun or entertainment on the other. Informed opinion about the effect of TV violence varies widely, perhaps because of the deliciously secretive nature of the subject. But the northern villages, which have only recently been exposed to TV, make excellent subjects for study, as raunchy TV from satellites and trashy videos are about the only variable that has been introduced to them in recent years.

But let me tell you about several incidents I was a part of, even if only peripherally as a prosecutor. Decide for yourself if they justify censorship.

In 1985, Fred Jamieson was a harum-scarum lad of seventeen or eighteen who lived in a sort of communal existence with a variety of relatives in a subsidized house in Minaki. The welfare authorities would have liked to get rid of most of the hangers-on, as they were parasites, but as they were all related to the primary tenant who was clearly deserving of public assistance, it was decided to let them stay. It didn't really matter, as wherever they were they would have been on the public teat. It was simply a matter of which particular teat they would be hanging on. There were a number of such households in Minaki, most of them with a few disaffected teenagers in their midst.

Describing the lifestyle of the Minaki teenagers presents difficulties, the main reason being that generalizations may not be accurate. They are, after all, individuals and not an amorphous mass. But we have to start somewhere. I apologize to those teenagers who rose above their circumstances. Fred Jamieson was not one of them.

Typically the Minaki teenagers, long since dropped out of school, lived together several in a room. Fred was lucky, as he only shared his room with one other boy, a cousin of about his own age. The day usually started around noon, when the teenagers pulled on their boots (like many of the denizens of Minaki they usually slept fully dressed) and rummaged the kitchen for food scraps. Perhaps an adult would send them to the store for a loaf of stale bread and a package of sliced baloney. Life was certainly not exciting.

Afternoons and evenings were spent aimlessly wandering from house to house and watching TV. The teenagers' favorite channel was the Playboy Channel, or any other channel that showed a lot of skin. They also enjoyed snuff flicks like The Texas Chainsaw Massacre, but no one recalled Fred Jamieson being any more interested than any other teenager, male or female. For what it is worth, Fred had a huge and very explicit centerfold on his wall, although at the time none of his companions attached any importance to it.

That was the shape of Fred's life when three-year-old Annie Kelly went missing one day in the fall of 1985. Perhaps more accurately, she just didn't show up where she normally did. This was not unusual, however, as by tradition and culture Native children are free to wander their communities, and are welcome in all homes. It is an attractive custom, but it can create problems in the modern world. Indeed, it resulted in Annie's death.

The adults in Annie's life were not concerned, not at first. Later in the day, just before dark, a house-to-house search was commenced. All the houses in the neighbourhood were canvassed, but no one had seen Annie.

By the following day the police became involved, and every person in the community was questioned, including Fred Jamieson. The police, or responsible adults, searched in and under every building, shack, woodshed and outhouse, still with no results.

In the search, particular attention was paid to vacant buildings. One young officer remembered pushing his way into an unlocked shack temporarily vacated by its normal occupant, who was a guest of the province for the time being at the Kenora jail. In the gloom he saw a pile of rags in the corner…but it surely wasn't large enough to conceal the body of a child. He went on to his next assigned area.

Several days passed, and still Annie had not been found. When the search was repeated it was a clear, bright day, and the light in the absentee owner's shack was much better. The little pile of rags, which was ignored the first time around, turned out to be the body of Annie Kelly. She had been sexually abused and strangled, probably right where she was found.

Eventually someone remembered having seen Fred Jamieson walking up the road with Annie on the day she went missing. The police at last had something to work with. At first he denied knowing anything about Annie, but the police let him stew for a day or two. Over a period of time little cracks appeared in his story, until finally he was so confused he just gave up.

Fred Jamieson was convicted of murder and sent away for a long while.

Did his exposure to trash TV, and the centerfold on the wall of his room, play a part in the crime?

At the risk of being called a fuddy-duddy, or out of date, I would have to say that it did.

Another case of harmful fantasy occurred in the village of Grassy Narrows, near Kenora, shortly after the advent of television. I have only my memory to refresh me on this one, no file notes or brief. Nevertheless, I am confident that I am accurate on the general story, if not on the finer details.

Julia Penner was a Pennsylvania Mennonite sent to relieve one of the mission schoolteachers at Grassy Narrows, who was away for a few weeks. Julia was young and nubile, but would have been horrified to think she was a turn-on to young Elvis Keesic.

Elvis lived with a number of relatives in a shack in the bush just behind the teacherage, and he would watch for Julia undressing at night, often with some of the other aimless teenagers who lived in the cabin. He watched and he fantasized. Sometimes he would turn to a skin flick channel and watch the antics of the girls and young women for hours at a time, dreaming Julia's face onto the squirming bodies on the screen…it seemed that white women liked their sex rough. Increasingly Elvis devoted himself to planning how he was going to oblige Julia Penner in her presumed longing for a tumble with him.

One winter night Elvis took some of his precious welfare money and bought a mickey from a taxi driver. He was alone in the house, so did not have to share his whiskey. Before long he was blotto. Taking a sharp filleting knife from the kitchen drawer, he plodded through the snow, past Julia's window, and around to the door. Banging on the door with his fist, he demanded to be let in. Julia, of course, had more sense than to open the door. "Open the door you fuckin' bitch," he called.

"Go away, there is nothing for you here," Julia replied as calmly as she could.

Elvis hadn't really expected immediate co-operation from Julia, although he was far from realistic about his ultimate expectations. One blow with Julia's wood splitting axe destroyed the latch on the door. As Julia backed away in terror he severed the safety chain with a second blow.

Julia was petrified, but she stood her ground, glaring defiance. "Get out," she said as forcefully as she could. "Get out right now or I'll have the police on you!"

"There won't be no police here," snarled Elvis, as he snatched the phone from the wall and tossed it into a corner, wires and all.

Dropping the axe and advancing towards Julia, Elvis pulled the stiletto-like filleting knife from his belt. These knives are exceptionally sharp and dangerous, and two or three can be found in almost every rural Canadian home. "We're gonna fuck," he said between quick intakes of breath. Julia was even more beautiful than he had fantasized...God, she was better than the girls on television.

Julia did not reply, but backed slowly through the hanging curtain into the bedroom part of the little square-timbered cabin. Elvis followed closely, pressing the point of the knife at the base of her throat.

"Take that thing off," demanded Elvis, flicking the point of the knife at a fold of Julia's nightie.

"No, I won't," Julia spat at him, "and you'd better get out or there will be a lot of trouble for you."

"You want to fight about it, eh?" Elvis' breath was coming fast, as he stared at her. He was inflamed now to the point of madness. "I know all about you white women. You want it rough, I'll give it to you rough." As he spoke he reached out and, still holding her at knifepoint, he fetched her a blow to the side of her head that sent her reeling against the wall. He was on her in an instant, severing the straps of her nightie with his razor sharp knife. Before she could recover her wits the nightie fell to the floor, leaving her completely naked and vulnerable.

Elvis was mesmerized by what he saw. It was just like in the skin flicks — a beautiful girl, breasts heaving, at the mercy of her assailant, quivering with anticipation. He did not trouble to note that Julia's quivering might have arisen from terror, not anticipation. The scenario was unfolding just as Elvis had fantasized.

It was all there, except for one thing: Julia had no intention of submitting to Elvis. Her continued resistance was not part of his dream.

Elvis Keesic, who had mastered hundreds of women in his fantasies, would teach this stupid woman about pain. She would soon beg him to take her.

With his left hand Elvis held Julia by the throat, immobilizing her against the wall. Taking his time, he deliberately carved a line of X's high on her breasts, right across her chest. She sobbed once, but didn't cry out.

The sight of blood did something to Elvis. Julia read death in his blurry eyes and on his whiskey-laden breath. With all her might she brought a knee up into his groin. Dropping the knife, Elvis sank to the floor with a groan. Julia ran by him and out into the snow, leaving a stream of blood drops and bare footprints. Down the path she ran, oblivious to her nakedness or the cold, screaming as she went, arriving at the door of the other teacherage.

I don't remember the real name of the missionary teacher behind the door, and if I did I wouldn't use it. But he heard Julia's screams and opened the door to her. As she ran in, the lady of the house phoned the police, who were just two hundred yards away from the mission school. The missionary slammed the door and barred it just as Elvis came charging around the end of the cabin, Julia's axe in hand.

Julia's knee to the groin had infuriated Elvis, although it had not disabled him for long. In a white-hot fury he yelled, "Open the fuckin' door and send that woman out, or I'll kill you all."

A deer rifle belonging to another resident missionary was available, but the man of the house refused to consider using it. He stalled for time. "What do you want with Julia?" he yelled through the door.

"You know what I want with her. She is my woman. She has to do what I want." Elvis was at the peak of his frenzy, not caring about or even considering the consequences of his actions. He sobbed with rage, or frustration. "Open the door or I'll break it down with this here axe," and to emphasize his threat he swung it at the door, with a terrific crash.

The effect on the people inside was stunning. The missionary's two young children clung to their mother, who stood like a statue in the middle of the floor. The missionary did nothing. Julia hissed at him, "Mr. Peters, for goodness sake, load the gun. Look what that animal has done to me already. He'll kill your children too if you don't do something." Opening the top of the housecoat Mrs. Peters had hastily thrown over her, she pointed to the bloody row of X's on her chest. He recoiled as if he had been bitten. Still he did nothing, seemingly paralyzed.

Outside Elvis paced in the snow, and raged. "Send her out, or I'll come in after her," he shouted again. There was no response from inside. Raising the axe, Elvis struck repeatedly at the door, splintering the heavy planks. He paused for a moment to inspect his handiwork, not seeing the shadow that materialized at the corner of the house.

Elvis struck again at the door just as a police officer leaped out of the darkness. The police officer slipped on the icy path just short of Elvis, and the two of them went down, Elvis on top, the axe still in his hand.

"Drop it or I'll shoot!" yelled the second officer who could only see a tangle of arms and legs in the dark, and the glint of the axe in the squirming mass. He knew that he was taking a chance by shooting in the dark, but because of the axe, he felt he had no choice. Aiming at a portion of the heap that he hoped was the arm of the axe man, he fired a single shot from his service revolver.

Elvis let out a piercing scream, as much for the sudden destruction of his fantasy as for the pain of the .38 caliber hole in his shoulder.

Julia stepped by the still paralyzed missionary and pushed the splintered door open. "You got here just in time," she said to the police.

A small army of social workers and do-gooders came to Elvis' aid. There were, of course, pleas of guilty to the several charges laid by the Crown. Julia was not seriously hurt by her injuries and was soon forgotten by the do-gooders. In the subtle way that often happens when society's values become skewed, efforts were made to persuade his lawyer to portray Elvis Keesic as the victim. In mitigation of sentence it was argued that Julia had led Elvis on, and that the influence of television was the real culprit. Nevertheless, Elvis was sentenced to spend several years in jail over this episode.

One is compelled to wonder if the lurid pornographic TV images played a part in Elvis' fantasies. Even if they did, Elvis still had the choice to break the law or not to break the law. The direction he took was his own choosing, and he made the wrong choice.

One bitter cold day in 1991 I found myself taking refuge in the police building at Atikwa Bay, that being a name I have coined to disguise the true identity of the village. I shared the living room with a young girl of about ten whose mother was cleaning the cells at the other end of the building while the little girl was watching TV.

Trying to have a little chat with the child, but having exhausted all our mutually understood words in English or Ojibway in five minutes, I turned to see what she had been watching. Lo and behold, the screen was filled with naked women (white) moaning and groaning in the throes of sexual ecstasy. The little girl managed to convey to me that her family watched that sort of thing all the time.

I have always been a sucker for little girls, but not to the extent that I automatically believe what they say.

Wandering down the hall past piles of parkas and mounds of snowy boots, I came to a wide spot where the girl's mother was having a cup of coffee with the cell guard and a prisoner. Launching into a dissertation on the evils of the exposure of children to pornographic television, I expected — I don't know what I expected — but I got cold indifference from the mother, who was not forthcoming at all. I think I ended my tirade with something like "Do you want your child to believe that is the way people on the outside act in real life?"

When the lady did not answer, the cell guard said, "If she could understand you she would say, "Yes, why not, that's the way white women act, isn't it?" "Anyways," piped a voice from a nearby cell, "everybody fucks. What's wrong with that?" They went on to explain that the chief controlled the community satellite dish, and if the chief wanted to watch something, the whole community was obliged to watch it too.

I retired in dismay to the living quarters where the child sat, enthralled by the gyrating bodies on the screen.

Duty called. I commenced to study the briefs for the cases that were to come before the court the following day, noting that a number of them were serious sexual assaults on children and family members, and noting that the victims had no community support whatsoever. I knew that most of the accused people would be acquitted, but I did not know whom to blame for this sad state of affairs.

Some time later, perhaps a year or so, I attempted to form a women's support group in Atikwa Bay, but was only able to recruit a few half-hearted members. Eventually I came to understand that a women's support group and a campaign against assaults on women was simply not on the agenda of the people of Atikwa Bay.

In Atikwa Bay, the women still look down at the ground and scurry by quickly when they meet a man on the path.

I no longer go there or attempt to intervene in their lives.

27: Airplanes and Feather Boas

I may have said it before, but just in case, I will say it again. There is a fine line between bragging and complaining, thus accounting for the absence of hero stories in this book. Call it bragging or complaining, but I have to tell you about several incidents that occurred after I learned to fly — not to just steer the airplane around on a clear day, but to use it as a tool to reach otherwise inaccessible or distant places.

At first every flight was a shake of the feather boa. After a few years, as my skills improved, I probably became a better pilot, as I didn't take as many chances. Make your own judgment as to whether I am bragging or confessing in the following anecdotes.

In the year 1972 the legal profession had not yet caught on to what a gold mine the Indian Reserves could be. The result was that many reserves did not have good advice, or sometimes any advice, about their business affairs. They were forced to stumble through their transactions with woeful results. From time to time I tried to fill the gap as a public service.

As it happens I was the regular prosecutor for the Armstrong court, even though Armstrong was in the District of Thunder Bay, under the supervision of Vic Ibbetson. Gull Bay was a large reserve south of Armstrong, and its citizens were also served by that court. I found it convenient to ride the CN passenger train east 165 miles over to Armstrong after every fourth Tuesday court at Sioux Lookout, or to fly in from Kenora or Dryden.

The chief of the Gull Bay Band was in the dock at one of these Armstrong courts. Looking abashed and deferential, he asked to speak to me when the court was over. I led him to the kitchen in the rooming house we were using as a courthouse. Settling in to listen to what I thought would be a complaint about the trial, which had resulted in his losing his driver's licence for impaired driving, I was surprised to learn that his complaint was about a business matter. He felt that the Hudson's Bay store at Gull Bay was gouging his band members. He wanted to know how the band could go about forcing the company to sell the store to the band. He gave me a few facts and figures off the top of his head, and I promised to meet with his council in one month, the day before the next Armstrong court.

A month from Tuesday was a beautiful day in Sioux Lookout, my departure point. There were no weather reports for the Lake Nipigon area, 165 miles east, which included both Armstrong and Gull Bay. Nevertheless I felt justified in flying without positive knowledge of the weather ahead in view of the beautiful, cloudless day. As the day was getting on I decided to fly directly to Gull Bay without stopping at Armstrong. As I circled the village once or twice I noticed that very little had changed since the night thirty years previously when Alex Langila and I huddled together in the cuddy of the *Ogemah*.

Taxiing up to the main dock at Gull Bay I had a feeling that something was wrong. Only a few children appeared to help me tie the airplane up. Ordinarily there would have been hordes of children and adults. When the chief did not show up I gave a kid a quarter to run and tell the chief I was waiting for him on the dock. His non-appearance was odd, because I knew that the whole village had heard me fly over.

Eventually, after a very long wait, the chief appeared, walking slowly. He was not attended by the expected retinue of councilors. The sky was beginning to cloud over, so I was becoming antsy.

"Hello, Chief. I'm here to talk about the Hudson's Bay store. Let's go where we can talk."

"I can't find my councilors."

This was a serious problem.

"Well, let's go up to your house and wait for them there." I knew from a previous visit that he had a good-sized front room.

"You can't just walk around the reserve. People might not like it. This is welfare day and a lot of people are liquored up. And besides, my old lady don't like strangers in the house. They make trouble."

I was beginning to understand that the chief simply did not want me around, but I was determined to salvage the meeting if I could. It was growing obvious that I was going to have to stay the night, and I was supremely p-o'd at the lack of action by the chief.

"Okay, then, I'll stay overnight in the school house. I've got a .45 here (opening my coat to show my shoulder holster) and I don't think anyone will bother me."

"Maybe not, maybe not, but I can't guarantee your plane will be safe. Them drunks might do something to it in the night."

I thought he might be threatening me, not merely giving me a warning. The writing was now on the wall, in great big letters.

I took off directly into the full moon that was rising behind the patchy clouds. I hadn't even had the opportunity to tell the chief that the Hudson's Bay Company was prepared to sell the store and contents to the band at cost, having made a profit in only one of the last thirty years.

Night flying on floats is absolutely not done, but I thought I had to do it, as staying the night in Gull Bay did not appear to be an option. I would have preferred to go north to Armstrong, but the sky looked threatening over that way. Instead I detoured to Disraeli Lake, a few miles to the southwest, which I had known as a temporary tower man the summer I was thirteen. I glided in, nose high with full flaps and a little power, making a perfect landing. Good luck or good management? I shot the lock off the forestry cabin door and spent a comfortable night in a bed.

In the morning I flew northwest to intercept the Armstrong road, and tied up at a convenient spot. Hoofing it through the bush with my briefcase and a couple of gas cans, I emerged out on the road and managed to thumb down the police paddy wagon, which was heading to Armstrong with prisoners. In the late afternoon, after court, an obliging lawyer, John Erickson, drove me back south to the place I had noted by the road, and helped me to lug my full gas cans back to the machine. It was near dark when I tied up at home in Kenora.

The feather boa had quite enough shaking for the time being.

On another occasion my friend Charlie Fisher, the first Native justice of the peace in Ontario, flew with me to Armstrong in a rented Cessna 170B, the same one that I had used on the trip previously described. This was a good machine, the difference from a simple Cessna 170 being that it had larger flaps than a 170 and utilized a 166-horsepower Franklin engine instead of the less powerful Lycoming or Continental engines ordinarily installed. We needed that extra power, because Charlie and I each weighed over 200 pounds, and I was in the habit of carrying a lot of gear when on bush flights.

The trip went well until the third day. I had detoured by Thunder Bay to look after a court for the Crown at that location and was intending to head back to Kenora in the afternoon. Alas, a large, forbidding, black cloud loomed on the horizon. I had learned that evil lurks in such clouds, and one must fly well clear of the end of any cloud that is shaped like an anvil. I changed direction to fly further south of the dark monster. The closer I came to it, the farther south I had to fly.

I guess I just didn't fly far enough around the tip of the anvil, or perhaps I should have flown around the other end of the cloud, for all of a sudden I was picked up as if by a giant hand, and sucked right up into the cloud. I stuffed the nose down, but still went up like an express train. Hail rattled off the horizontal surfaces in an earsplitting din. I remembered my dad describing a similar experience, so I throttled back and resigned myself to riding the elevator through the storm. In two or three minutes we were through the cloud and in clear air at 10,000 feet. I looked over at Charlie and noticed his hands were white and shaking on his knees. My own hands were the same. Small aircraft have been known to be sucked up and spit out at altitudes up to 25,000 feet in such clouds.

We flew north for a good half hour before encountering the Thunder Bay–Fort Frances highway. Landing for a smoke, or two or three, we recovered our courage, and flew to Fort Frances. Taking fuel was a frequent necessity, as the starboard wing tank could only be half filled.

I always liked traveling with Charlie, because as a reformed alcoholic he tended to keep me on the straight and narrow. He never preached to me about booze, but always poured for me, even if he was abominably stingy with the amount.

"Here you are," he said that night in our Fort Frances hotel room. "Drink it up. You earned it today."

Chalk up another one for the feather boa.

My last aviation story, at least the last one I am going to tell you about, was in the Buccaneer, a four-place amphibian with a pusher engine and wheels that retracted into the wings. The pilot could look back and see that the main wheels were up or down, as required, but the only indicator of the position of the nose wheel was a dinky little convex mirror out on the port wingtip float. Looking at it, you could theoretically see the nose wheel and determine its position. Trouble was, the convex mirror made the nose wheel appear to be way out on the horizon. It would tell you if the wheel was down, for a runway landing if you could see it, or up, for a water landing if you couldn't; but it didn't tell you if it was locked in position.

The trip started in Winnipeg, where I picked up the aircraft, and lasted about ten days. I flew to Kenora, landing on the Lake of the Woods. The next leg was to Oshkosh, Wisconsin, for the EAA (Experimental Aviation Association) fly-in, with sons Ted and Mike and their friend Will Scutt as passengers. I had a great affection for Wittman Field at Oshkosh, recalling the time several years previously when I had landed with 200 other airplanes in the circuit, thereby scaring myself silly. We were well loaded with sleeping bags and gear with which we bedded down under the wings on the field. Several more days found us winging our way directly across Lake Michigan, then north to Sault Ste Marie, where the boys caught the bus home to Kenora.

The last leg of that day was from Sault Ste Marie to Sudbury. Landing on Ramsay Lake was a breeze, but I was astounded to be turned away from Austin Airways' base. As night fell, I taxied around in the dark until a kindly citizen came out in his boat and led me to a safe tie-down place, and gave me a place to sleep.

My boss, Herb Langdon, met me in Sudbury and accompanied me on the business part of the trip. We gassed up at the Sudbury airport, then flew north to Moosonee, landing on the prepared strip. That night I slept in a proper bed in a hotel, the first in several days. Herb, who was an ex-paratrooper, said he didn't care where he slept, but I did. I really appreciated comfort. Still do, for that matter. The years I spent sleeping on an air mattress or a bed of twigs were long gone, and I didn't miss that part of life in the bush.

On the following day we took time off and went exploring over on Moose Factory Island. This island in the huge river that drains thousands of square miles of the Hudson Bay lowlands was an early fur trade outpost and contains visible reminders of its romantic past. A hand-operated fur press still stood outside a down-at-the-heels square timber strong house that was an original fur trade warehouse. We also explored an ancient Anglican church still in use, which had holes bored around the floor to let the spring flood water flow out. We refrained from attempting to explore the huge, modern Zone hospital, which sat in lonesome splendor among the shabby but picturesque village houses. We had an excellent meal before hitting the sack that night.

The following day presented typical Hudson Bay lowland weather, being windy, rainy and dark, with low visibility. I elected to fly anyway, knowing there were no hills or high trees anywhere around, and very few towers to cause problems to low flying aircraft.

The first stop was Attawapiskat, where I took on fuel and renewed acquaintance with Roy Turner, the Hudson's Bay post manager, whom I had known years before at another post. Procuring the fuel was a matter of walking into the village accompanied by clouds of mosquitoes and blackflies, renting a truck, finding the man who had the key to the warehouse, loading a drum of fuel, driving back to the airport, pouring in as much as the main tank could hold, returning the truck to its owner, and walking back to the airstrip.

We made it as far as the Sutton River that day, tying up at a shack owned by the Ministry of Natural Resources. The Sutton River is world famous for its lake trout and speckled trout fishing, but we caught nothing. Even so, the steak and fresh mushrooms we brought with us, and which Herb cooked over the wood stove, made a darn fine dinner.

The next day, a Sunday, we flew the remaining 50 miles or so over the tundra to Winisk, seeing two polar bears on the mud flats quite near the village. I wondered if the children of Winisk were safe with those brutes prowling about, but was informed that they never came right into the village, and but seldom onto the abandoned radar base where we had landed.

Because of the business that brought me to Winisk, I expected to have to cross the broad delta of the meandering Winisk River, meeting the chief on his own turf, right in the village. I was quite surprised when the caretaker of the hangar where I had parked the aircraft told us the chief was holed up in the one of the few remaining serviceable buildings of the defunct base, and that he probably would not want to see us. Translated, that meant he was drunk. My mission was actually benign and non-threatening. Judicial district boundaries were in the process of being redrawn. I had been delegated to sound out the chiefs and councils in the affected areas, and I needed to find out if the people of Winisk were happy being part of the District of Kenora, or would they rather their justice be administered out of Cochrane.

Herb stayed in the truck, chatting with the driver, while I went to the door to find the chief. Fear and hostility poured out of the door of the plywood building like a cloud. When I asked for the chief, a bedraggled woman told me in halting English that he was asleep, and I should go away. I stood there arguing for a few minutes, to no avail. Herb remained in the truck throughout.

Suddenly two shots sounded from behind the building. I had no idea who was shooting, or at what, and I glanced at the truck to reassure myself, or...goodness only knows why I looked, but I did. There was deaf Herbie, stuffing his pipe, oblivious to what was going on. The truck driver motioned me to hurry, and I was pleased to oblige. The shots might have been quite unconnected with the business at hand; it was likely, however, that someone was sending us a message. We roared off at high speed back to the hangar, not waiting to hear more shots. The truck driver, who was shaking like a leaf, advised me that the decision to leave was a wise one.

I had tweaked the feather boa, though I had not really given it a good shake.

Since it was futile at that point to attempt to engage the chief in any discussions, we decided to get on our way next morning and continued on to Fort Severn, tracking the coastline all the way. On taking off from the airstrip I duly noted that I had some trouble raising the flaps and wheels, but the hydraulic pressure gauge showed green, so I was not overly concerned. At Fort Severn I acquired some hydraulic fluid with which to give the Buccaneer's system a drink.

The reception given us at Fort Severn was in direct contrast to our reception at Winisk. The chief's wife served tea and cookies and we calmly discussed the merits of the District of Kenora as opposed to the District of Cochrane. We were made welcome in a private home for the night. There was no booze in evidence at the village.

The following day, Tuesday, we flew to Big Trout Lake, landing on the water. We took fuel, and once again there was trouble with the flaps on take-off. I should have twigged to the fact, but did not, that there was an internal leak in the hydraulic system. At Red Lake, another water landing, we took on fuel, and again experienced flap problems. Taking off immediately, I could not get the flaps fully down. Landing on the lake at Kenora was hairy, as the aircraft is supposed to have full flaps for every landing and takeoff. I knew I could control the machine without using flaps, but I reckoned without the necessity of operating the nose wheel with hydraulic pressure for a wheel landing.

The takeoff at Kenora seemed to require half of Lake of the Woods, without flaps. Of course I had given no thought to the wheels since the take-off from the airstrip at Fort Severn earlier in the day. The Buccaneer was urgently required in Winnipeg, and since there was plenty of daylight left I had decided to deliver the machine back to the rental agency, Pace Aviation, without further delay. I traded Herb Langdon off for Kelly Cummine, a young lad eager for his first airplane ride, and flew westward

Securing the Buccaneer on the shores of the Sutton River, August 1977. Photo courtesy of H.W. Langdon.

quite unconcerned, a satisfactory northern tour behind me, and confident in my ability to deal with the flap problem one more time for my last landing. I noted that the machine had been sluggish on take-off, but that could have been because of the flaps, or maybe it was just my technique.

It all caught up to me at Winnipeg.

I made a standard approach to the main runway at Stevenson Field, selecting wheels down as I turned on final. The mains came down and locked, but there was that damned little mirror out on the float that was supposed to tell me about the nose wheel. I peered at it in an effort to make out the nose wheel. It looked like it was down, but was it locked? I had to look away in order to pay some attention to the attitude of the airplane. Suddenly the machine sank heavily, and I applied power to hold it in the air. But it had a mind of its own. In spite of the extra speed it proceeded to squat on the runway like a pregnant duck. There was terrific screeching of metal, and I realized that the nose wheel had retracted or folded up, or perhaps it was never fully down, and the belly had ripped open where it skidded on the runway. I had the presence of mind to check the flaps, noting that they were only partly down.

Chaos! Screeching sirens! Curses over the radio from following aircraft that had to go around again!

I walked sadly around the airplane, kicking bits and pieces of aluminum off to one side. Kelly quietly said, "That wasn't a normal landing, was it?"

When the smoke had cleared and a proper assessment completed, it came to light that the hydraulic fluid I had put in at Fort Severn was the wrong type, and had caused some internal hydraulic seals to leak, which in turn was responsible for the problem with the flaps and the nose wheel. Fortunately, Pace Aviation's insurance picked up the tab for the damage.

It had been a good trip until the last ten seconds. The feather boa had once again reared its head and had been well shaken. On returning to Kenora I decided to leave it alone for a while.

28: Some Call it ESP

A friend once talked me into visiting a man with a teapot and a deck of cards. I don't really believe in psychic powers, preferring to believe that some people have a form of intelligence that allows them to perceive things that pass by the rest of us without being noticed. Call it a "power" if you like, but the word is a little too close to the term "mind reading" to suit me. "Extra-sensory perception" may describe this special aptitude as well as anything.

As a boy I had had an uncanny experience with a crystal ball lady at a children's birthday party. She told me all about a flying expedition in the arctic upon which my father was engaged at the time. The birthday party and the crystal ball lady were in Augusta, Georgia, and the event made a lasting impression on me, the more so because, as far as I know to this day, there was no way she could have learned anything about me or my father in advance. I had tagged along at the last minute with a friend of the birthday kid's and didn't know any of the people who were there, and none of them knew anything about me. In 1988 I was, therefore, quite receptive to the urging of a friend who knew I was looking in my own memory and elsewhere for information about another flying adventure my father had in the year after I was born, and about which he had told me. Yes, I admit it. I let my friend drag me off to a fortune-teller.

The old house was on a crummy street in downtown Toronto, just a few blocks from the Yonge St. sin strip. Little kids looked down at the pavement when they passed you on the street, squashing over an extra few inches as they did so. That was a tip-off about what kind of neighbourhood it was. On the porch of the house we were going to there was a hand-printed sign: "Cards. Readings."

The dark and dingy interior was no more congenial than the street outside. The 1920's vintage wallpaper was peeling and smudged. Decades of accumulated cooking smells seeped from the walls of the hall and kitchen.

A bored girl who should have been in school led us to a cubicle furnished with a small table and two chairs. We sat down, and she soon reappeared with a teapot and two cups. "We're here to see Mr. Simon," said my friend. The girl nodded and faded into the darkness of the corridor. Perhaps it was a good thing it was so dark in that shabby place, as I couldn't inspect the teacup for cleanliness.

Mr. Simon eventually showed up, bringing a little stool along to sit on. "You've been here before," he said to my friend.

"That's right, and you helped me then. Now I want you to help my friend. I thought you might be able to put him in the right frame of mind so he could recall some things his father told him." My friend was about to say more, but Mr. Simon held up his hand and became thoughtful. I looked him over as he sat there, noting that he was in his mid-fifties and very unwashed, matching the ambience of the house and street.

The fortune-teller suddenly got to his feet. "Drink your tea. I'll be back." When he came he had a deck of tarot cards with which he fiddled nervously. He picked up my cup and looked at it, twirling it in his hands and muttering. Occasionally he stirred the cards on the table with his fingers.

I should have kept my mouth shut, of course, but not being a true believer I felt obliged to contribute to the exercise. I said something to the effect that his knowledge, or power, or whatever, was all in his own head, so why didn't he get on with it and never mind the tea leaves and the cards. He laughed, and spoke to me directly for the first time. His voice was that of a cultured Englishman, which was in complete contradiction to his grimy appearance. "Sir, you don't understand. The tea leaves are for my own benefit, not yours. They psych me up and put me in a receptive frame of mind." He didn't say what the tarot cards were for.

Mr. Simon ruminated for a moment or two, and then went on. "I sense, for example, that your father was a voyager in small vessels, and that he voyaged to remote places. You wish to recall what he told you about one of those trips, perhaps a voyage to northern latitudes. Perhaps you want to write about it. There is something odd about the vessel…" His voice trailed off.

I was amazed. More than that, I was completely astounded. The voyage of my father in which I was interested was indeed to northern latitudes, to the Yukon Territories and Alaska, to be precise. It happened a few months after I was born. His "small vessel" was one of a group of five Eastman Sea Rover Flying Boats, which took off and landed on the water. They were on a gold seeking expedition. The fortune-teller's perception was close enough to give me a strange prickly feeling in the back of my neck, a feeling that I have experienced only in the presence of great physical danger or when confronted with something totally unexplainable.

A bosomy middle-aged lady, still pretty, walked by our cubicle and Mr. Simon motioned her in. Gold teeth flashed from a dark face capped with curly black hair. I distinctly recall that her underwear was visible in her cleavage. It was men's long woolen winter underwear sewn together at the top. The image of the similarly unwashed crystal ball lady at the garden party of my childhood churned into my mind, and I wondered if the unwashed state was an essential attribute of fortune-tellers.

The blowzy woman ran her fingers around in the cards, muttering in the same way as had Mr. Simon. "Yes, I see water here, and a funny little ship. This man seems to be interested in a trip someone close to him took in his little ship. I think the voyage ended in disaster." Her voice dropped and she left abruptly.

Mr. Simon would have given me more, but I couldn't take it. My three dollars had bought me a fascinating fifteen minutes, and I walked away reflecting moodily that there was a great deal science did not yet know about the human mind.

Neither Mr. Simon nor the blowzy lady had told me much of value concerning my father's adventures, but what I learned about the operation of the human mind more than made up for it.

Perhaps I should have mentioned earlier on that the crystal ball lady of my childhood party in Augusta had focused on the fact that my dad was away on a northern expedition at the time, not in a flying boat, but a Waco floatplane. The flying boat expedition had been to the Yukon in 1932, but the Waco floatplane expedition, which was happening even as I was speaking to the lady at the children's party, was to the barren lands of the Northwest Territories.

"*Monsieur. Monsieur*. I believe this gentleman wishes to speak to you."

I turned around to the kindly priest just behind me in the fast food lineup at the Pearson International Airport, which I still think of as Malton Airport. For once I was well ahead of time, looking forward to a few minutes to collect my thoughts and put the effects of a hectic day behind me. Busy airports are harrowing experiences, and the few spare minutes were a luxury to me.

"*Monsieur,* this man has been trying to get your attention. I think he wants some help."

I looked down at a little old elf in his eighties, who was tapping my elbow with one hand and dragging a large suitcase with the other. He was plainly agitated, and I wondered why his airline had not given him some assistance, and why he had not turned to the priest behind me for help. I made a deliberate effort to clear my mind of little wrinkles and negative thoughts, remembering that it is my destiny to be accosted by strangers who require help of some sort. Put it down to kismet, ESP or whatever, but it has happened to me far too often to be mere coincidence. I pulled myself together and shifted my large package in order to give him my attention.

"How can I help you?" I said, forcing my voice to sound cheerful.

"I knew you'd help me. You know all about airplanes. Say, I'm just about done in." He spoke in a quavery voice.

"We'd better get you some coffee and you can tell me what the problem is."

I eased him into the line ahead of me and looked back to see if those behind me were going to object. I saw nothing but smiles. Maybe people aren't so bad after all.

Negotiating my parcel, my club bag, the old gent, his suitcase, a cardboard cup of coffee, and a too-hot cup of tea, was more than I could manage, and I was grateful to the priest for helping me to one of those little stand-up tables. *"Au revoir,"* he chirped as he disappeared into the crowd. A nice guy.

I'd better tell you about my special parcel. It was a large framed reproduction of a montage of paintings of aircraft used by the Ontario Provincial Air Service branch of the Department of Lands and Forests, as it was formerly called, in the development of the Canadian North. It was a gift from the Honorable Leo Bernier, then the Minister of Natural Resources. He had caught me eyeing it, and probably thought I was trying to liberate it from its position on one of the main walls in the elevator lobby of his floor in the Hepburn Block of the Parliament Buildings in Toronto. Cardboard and heavy brown paper shrouded it so that you couldn't tell from the outside what the package contained. My dad had flown many of the aircraft depicted, and in fact I had been a passenger in quite a few of them as a kid. I was a private pilot myself at the time of the airport encounter and had a serious interest in historic aircraft, particularly flying boats. But my new friend couldn't possibly have known any of this.

"I knew you'd help me," he said again. "I'm getting on in years, and only have three or four really good hours a day, and I've already had 'em for today." The old elf gasped for breath as he sipped his coffee.

I tried not to let him see that I was impatient.

Collage of the Ontario Provincial Air Service floatplanes from 1921.

"I'm supposed to be flying over to Europe on one of those bloody great jets, but I've lost my way in this damned maze of a building, and I don't know where to go next." His accent was distinctly Northern England. As he spoke he took a fistful of papers out of his inside blazer pocket, thrusting them into my not-too-eager hand.

"I don't really know all about airplanes," I said firmly, "and anyway, it's someone who knows about airports and traveling that you need to talk to." It was only partly true, as I figured in my own mind that I knew a hell of a lot about airplanes. In fact I also knew Terminal One like the back of my hand. But the old boy wasn't discouraged, and he shoved more papers at me.

The assortment of bills, receipts, shopping lists, and letters took my attention. And yes — there was a BOAC (British Overseas Airways Corporation) ticket envelope in there. He was ticketed to Manchester, with a stop at Prestwick, Scotland. A boarding pass fell to the floor. I looked at it. Flight time was right now.

"Take a last sip and hang on to my coat tail, 'cause we've got to run,"

I said as I scooped up our luggage. He did just that, and we lit out for the security gate. He hung on like a dog to a bone.

“Gangway!” I shouted as we ran through the crowd. “Make way for a late flyer!” There was a long lineup at the security gate, but people good-naturedly made way for us without complaint. I towed the old man right through the x-ray arch. They gave us both a perfunctory check with the wand, and pointed us down the corridor. We resumed our frantic rush to the BOAC departure gate.

“Mr. Alveston, where have you been? We’ve been calling for you on the PA system. I’ll see if the door has been closed yet. Perhaps you can get aboard after all.” The attendant’s voice had a trace of scold in it. I could understand why, but I didn’t say anything. She picked up the phone and stabbed frantically at the buttons. She spoke, and listened. The worry lines disappeared from her face. “It’s okay, there’s been a fifteen-minute delay. I’ll take you down shortly.”

While waiting I asked the traveler why he had singled me out for help. He looked a little crestfallen, or sheepish. His answer was peculiar, and many years later I still wonder about it. “Well, I could see that you know all about airplanes of course, and I knew you’d help me.”

I repeated that I didn’t know all about airplanes, and added that whatever I knew wasn’t much help in the circumstances. His face assumed a funny expression, as if he didn’t quite believe me.

I can’t really explain why I did it, but I slit the end of the paper covering my aircraft montage and slid it out just far enough for him to see what it was. There was a Grumman Widgeon in the picture and a Vickers Vedette down near the bottom. Just out of sight was an ancient Curtiss HS-2L. A Canso and a Loening flying boat were somewhere in the picture too. I didn’t tell him, but I had become passably competent at flying the Buccaneer amphibian myself, although there was no Buccaneer in the picture.

My friend’s face was transformed with delight. “Of course, of course! I knew it was something like that under the paper. I used to be in Clipper Ships with Pan Am. I was a radio operator on the Miami to Rio run, and I had a ground station in the Caribbean during the war. Give me your name and address and I’ll send you a book about flying boats from Manchester.”

As the BOAC lady led him down the ramp I felt a peculiar rising of the hairs on the back of my neck. Why did the old gentleman seek me out when there were hundreds of other more logical people he could have asked? How could he be so sure I would help him? How did he suspect what was in the brown paper package? How did he know of my interest in airplanes, particularly flying boats?

A few weeks later I got a card from my flying-boat man, as I think of him, mailed from Paris, but I never heard from him again.

For a person who doesn't believe in ESP and is extremely dubious about the whole subject of psychic phenomena, I seem to have been exposed to a number of unexplainable occurrences in the last half century. Equally unexplainable is the fact that all of these occurrences had something to do with airplanes or airports.

Several of these incidents were in my mind some years ago, and I put them down on paper, not knowing what their significance was, or what I would do with them. Today is a beautiful August day on Lake of the Woods, but storm clouds are threatening and the wind is picking up. Few boats are abroad. Erica is on a summer visit to Thunder Bay. I am alone on the island. I have lots of time to think as I slop green Cuprinol preservative on some dock planks.

I think back on the crystal ball lady at the birthday party in Augusta. I muse on the two rather unwashed fortune-tellers in Toronto, and I spend a moment in recall of the flying-boat man at Pearson International Airport.

These incidents are running through my mind when a Twin Otter on floats flies over, just above the trees. I speculate that it came from a nearby tourist camp, and is heading back to its base in Kenora. On the other hand, perhaps the pilot just likes to fly low! It is safe enough over Lake of the Woods. I let my mind wander over the many, many Twin Otter trips I had over the years, on wheels, skis, floats and tundra tires.

I don't like the wind and never did. Weird noises, probably the calls of sea gulls, float over the air and deflect my thoughts. I don't know why one particular Twin Otter trip keeps on returning to my mind, but it does. I set myself to deliberately remember the details as I pour more Cuprinol into the can. The damn stuff spatters so readily, and the stain won't wash out of clothing. The amorphous thought that has been trying to nudge its way out of my subconscious finally comes to the surface, like a chick about to break through an egg shell. I glance at it, but it retreats before I can fully grasp it. Annoyed with my inability to focus, I go on slopping Cuprinol on the planks.

In the early 1970s a village called Poplar Hill, some twenty-five miles downstream on the Berens River from Pikanjikum, came to official attention. The Department of Indian and Northern Affairs built a beautiful three-room school and a three-unit teacherage, and the local children promptly set about destroying them with .22's and .30-30's. The village closed ranks around the offenders, and the police were not able to learn anything useful.

As if to spite the authorities, even many of the older people set out on a course of deliberate lawlessness. One of the incidental crimes was the frequent break-in of the local store. One of these we could prove because the storekeeper, one Abe Skatch from a Manitoba reserve, was aggrieved and was not afraid to testify.

Getting the offenders to court was another matter. One effort at holding court in the village failed because of the menace of forest fires. On another occasion the malefactors took off for the bush as soon as the plane landed. Short of arresting everyone in the village and flying them out, it looked like we could never mount a trial. Eventually we managed to deal with a number of young offenders by taking them to Red Lake, but one young woman of seventeen or eighteen eluded the police for over a year, slipping away like a wraith whenever they appeared.

The police concocted a rather ingenious method of apprehending the girl. Towards the end of winter they learned that she had had a baby in Sioux Lookout and had returned to the village. It seemed unlikely that she would take off into the bush either with or without her baby. The plan was for the court party to fly in unannounced with the police, land as close to the shore as possible, and the police would run up and collar the young woman before she could hide or run away. We would take the storekeeper's evidence on the spot. The preparations were kept totally confidential so there would be no chance of anyone in Poplar Hill learning in advance of the court plans. I suppose nothing is certain but death and taxes, but I am absolutely certain there was no way the girl could have known what was in store for her, as there was not even radio contact with the village at the time. Not more than two or three days elapsed from the conception of the plan until we put it into action.

The fateful day arrived, and the Ministry sent a Twin Otter on tundra tires to pick us up. This was an unusual, but effective contraption, the nose wheel being on a wide ski with a slot in it, permitting the forward weight to rest on the ski or the wheel as required. The main wheels were huge, low pressure, doughnut tires. When the aircraft touched down it went — *poing! poing! poing!* — like a giant basketball. In a stiff breeze it might leap off after only two poings.

The pilot did his job perfectly, setting us down right at the edge of the village. Our policeman legged it out to the hovel occupied by the girl and her family, and had her at the door of the aircraft before the rest of the court party had clambered out. I recall noting that she did not seem perturbed.

We were all quite astonished to learn from duty counsel, who held a quick conference with his client while standing under the wing, under the watchful gaze of a police officer, that the girl intended to plead guilty. Given her several attempts to escape punishment we expected and were prepared for a trial. I read in the particulars while sitting on the wheel, and the judge, sitting in the main door, gave her a sentence of three months in the Kenora District Jail. Far from being upset by being parted from her new baby, the girl was quite placid about it.

Speaking a little English for the first time, she told us she would like us to land at Pikanjikum, where she had a sister, also nursing a baby, who had enough milk for two. The day was still young, and the pilot said there would be time to allow the girl to seek out her sister at Pik. We could fly back in the dark if necessary.

A ten-minute flight and *poing! poing! poing!* we were down on the ice at Pik, the tundra tires sitting astride a skidoo trail. Immediately the aircraft came to rest, a woman was at the door, speaking to our prisoner. Without saying very much she handed out her tiny baby in its *tikanagan*.

"Wait a moment now," said the judge. "These circumstances are highly unusual, and I think we have an obligation to see this baby is looked after. Just who is the woman taking the baby, and how do we know she will look after it?"

The girl looked at the floor, not meeting our eyes. She spoke in the halting voice of one who does not use the language often. "This is my sister. She has been waiting for us. I sent word to her by my brother on his snow machine last night, that I would be going to jail today, and to meet the airplane to take the baby."

The girl would answer no further questions, and conversation became impossible as we went *poing! poing! poing!* across the ice and became airborne. Was this the same phenomenon as those other incidents that so perplexed me?

I have finished working on the planks and gone into the cabin. I notice that my fingers are stained a bright green that will not come off with scrubbing. The darkening sky and rising wind look likely to turn into one of those earth-shaking thunderstorms that seem particularly spectacular on Lake of the Woods. I have eaten my solitary supper, cleared the table, and picked up a pen and paper.

29: A Vignette

At a band office adjacent to a highway in Northwestern Ontario:

Me: "Bojou, Chief and Councilors. My name is Ted Burton. I am the new Crown attorney for the District of Thunder Bay. I am driving to a court up the line and I thought it would be a good idea to drop in on the way by to get acquainted. I was lucky to find you people together at the same time. As a matter of fact, I used to live near here when I was a young lad. I probably knew some of your parents when I...blah, blah, blah."

A councilor: "Jeeze, I wonder if you could be my father!"
All: Much laughter.

Me: "But, but, but."

Second councilor: "My mother said she didn't know who my father is."

All: Much laughter and slapping of thighs.

Me: "But I want to say..."

Third councilor: "My mother told me my father was three guys on a fish tug. Was you on that fish tug?"

All: Much laughter. Guffaws. Fingers pointed in my direction.

Me: I think I'd better be going.

30: Boats

Some choices in life turn out to be building blocks for the future; some are definitely not to be repeated but lessons learned; and some lead to "feather boa" moments with the potential for disaster but which, once overcome, are a source of satisfaction and add to a reservoir of inner strength. I had the good fortune of being around in an age and environment that presented a variety of choices and experiences, and folks I encountered along the way taught me that there is almost always something of interest to be learned from others' perspective on matters.

Since my dad was a pilot, and many of his friends were bush pilots and other adventurous types, I developed an avid interest in airplanes at an early age, and liked nothing better than to hang around at the docks to watch takeoffs and landings, and to help with any manner of airplane-related chores. I eagerly listened to the men talking about flying, the challenges they faced and the narrow escapes. It was many years later, at thirty, that I got my pilot's license, and experienced first-hand the exhilaration, and the feather boa potential, of taking to the air.

Growing up as a forestry kid, messing around in boats came naturally as a pastime, and boats always figured as a part of my life. Once I had settled in Kenora, and made my home on Coney Island, they also became a necessity, and over the years and in a variety of boats I have navigated among the thousands of islands on Lake of the Woods. A body of water — any body of water — holds a special attraction, and there must be few in the world that can rival Lake of the Woods for scenic beauty.

With retirement came more time to pursue my interest in writing, among other things. I also felt an urge to embark on some type of adventure, and an opportunity soon presented itself. My son Michael assembled a crew of five to ferry a forty-foot trimaran sailboat from the Florida Keys to Thunder Bay, and I happily signed on. I had little sailing experience; however, shipboard duties soon sorted themselves out according to everyone's capabilities. There were some tense moments — sudden storms, navigation challenges, particularly in fog conditions in the commercial shipping lanes — which caused some consternation, and we were thankful for the auxiliary diesel engine on more than one occasion. The trip, along the Intracoastal Waterway, the Erie Canal and the Great Lakes, was an opportunity to view that part of the world from a unique vantage point, and to become acquainted with the cruising lifestyle, which appealed to me enormously.

Shortly afterwards, I had a stroke which knocked me flat. Instead of enjoying camp time, boating, and catching rides in friends' airplanes, I spent most of the summer in the hospital. I was lucky: I came out of it relatively intact, albeit with decreased mobility and energy, a strict medical program, and a new awareness of my own mortality. Erica and I resumed a more leisurely style of travel. There was some unfinished business to take care of in Florida. Relatives were visited, and my mother's ashes were interred in the historic little Euchee Valley cemetery, shaded by ancient magnolia trees, where her ancestors have been laid to rest for generations. Nearby are the amazingly white beaches and turquoise waters of the Gulf, where I had spent happy times as a youngster, surrounded by doting family members, long since gone. We stayed for a while in a part of Florida where amusement parks and fast food outlets had not yet proliferated, and where the folks who run the fishing boats feature the day's catch on their dinner specials.

We explored the Outer Banks of North Carolina, and returned with friends to Oshkosh for the annual Experimental Aircraft Association convention. In the heartland of the country, it draws enthusiasts from all over the world, and is a showcase for innovations in the continually evolving private aviation industry. I immersed myself in the sights and sounds of the world's largest fly-in gathering, and reflected on my earlier visits, when I had flown in as part of the swarm of airplanes jockeying for air space and a quick touchdown so as to get out of the way as fast as possible. However, my pilot's license was a thing of the past, having some years ago fallen victim to a medical examiner's pronouncement on the state of my ticker.

Now summer is ending on Lake of the Woods. The days are still warm and sunny, but there is a chill in the evening air. Labor Day weekend has come and gone, camps are boarded up, boats are hoisted up on lifts or turned upside down on the shore, and there is little traffic. The occasional boats going by are not the big flashy cruisers and the houseboats of summer, but the more utilitarian craft preferred by the lake people. Most of the leaves have fallen and what is left is golden and brittle and rustles in the wind. Tomorrow we will pack up and close the camp for another year.

I walked down to the dock after supper, and sat for a while watching a large beaver swim to shore from the next island. He either didn't see me or decided I posed no threat, as he dragged a poplar branch from the shore and swam back out with it. It was a long way to come for a stick, and there are plenty of trees where he came from. It must be simply that this is what he likes to do. A couple of loons were out on patrol, sounding their drawn-out call, answered in the distance like an eerie echo. The smell of wood smoke drifted down from the cabin. Earlier today a bear had made a stopover on the island in its foray for a food supply. It had rooted and scratched at a rotted log, hopeful of finding a mouthful of ants or beetles. As I made my way back to the cabin, the huge, full orange moon began to rise. Later we will stoke up the stove for the night and sit on the deck for a while and watch the stars and moonlight ripple on the water.

I paused on the step and looked around at the silhouette of shoreline and distant islands, and had a passing thought that this scene has remained and will continue unchanged over the centuries. Trees will sprout from seeds and grow into towering giants and shelter the young growth, and succumb to storms or old age, and new ones will take their place, just as the cycle of human life renews itself with each generation. It is a comforting thought, and it is all in the natural order of things.

Atikwa Bay

This was an open letter published in *Wawatay News* in the form of an editorial several years after I retired. I really hoped it would stir up some reaction among First Nations people, and was disappointed when it met a blank wall. A white administrator at the Zone Hospital in Sioux Lookout tried to have it refuted by another white writer on Native affairs, but he refused. One First Nations leader with whom I had not been on good terms for many years sent word by roundabout means that it was about time someone said these things to the First Nations of Northwestern Ontario. Other than that, nothing.

This editorial was printed in 1996 over the course of five editions in *Wawatay News,* a weekly paper slanted towards the First Nations people, printed in both English and in syllabics. *Atikwa,* or some variation of it, was the word used for caribou at one time. I am told that the caribou moved out early in the 19th century and were replaced by deer, which migrated to Northwestern Ontario from Minnesota. The word now applies to deer. I frequently use it as a place name to disguise a location.

Anicinabe translates literally to "human being" in the Ojibway, and is now used to mean Indian, as opposed to White. *Anicinabek* is the plural.

Letter to Atikwa Bay

Atikwa Bay is not, of course, a place that really exists. I have invented the name in order to preserve the feelings of the several villages at which this letter is really directed, not wishing to single them out by their proper names, thereby subjecting them to ridicule. I believe the villages I have selected will have no trouble in recognizing themselves, and it is my hope that they will examine their activities in the light of what I have to say. I assure the Anicinabek that I do not wish to insult or do injury, but only to cause certain of your people to think about how the actions of the older people on the reserve are affecting the youth. My remarks do not apply to every First Nations village.

There will probably be very little in this letter that is unfamiliar to you, and certainly nothing in it that the larger society does not talk about when no Anicinabek are listening. What is new is that I am putting these things out in the open for all to see in the hopes that you will talk about it among yourselves.

Why are your young people committing suicide? What can be done to make life better for them? Who should be responsible for improving their lives?

These questions are gnawing at the people of Canada's northern villages. I hope my way of confronting these questions will help when you consider the solutions to your problems. I undertake to speak the truth as I see it.

For many years I have heard the people of Atikwa Bay say their troubles are caused by booze and bootleggers, by a lack of policing, by courts that don't understand the people, and by schools that do not teach the things that children need to know. You say that the troubles that beset the community are always someone else's fault. Never have I heard the people of Atikwa Bay speak up and volunteer solutions to their own problems. Never have I heard the people say they are ready to make their own way to a better life.

What I hear is that it is not traditional, or within the culture of the people, for parents to interfere in the lives of their children, as if that would excuse the parents for their lack of interest. I hear that the teaching methods of modern schools are not suited to the culture of Ojibway children, as if that would excuse them for skipping school or not doing homework. I have observed that the people of Atikwa Bay do not want to come to court to testify against people charged with crime, not even against bootleggers or sexual abusers, because they say "It is not our way." In short, the people of Atikwa Bay simply refuse to be responsible for what happens to them, or to do anything that will make their lives better.

One result of this refusal to take responsibility is that the children have little structure or foundation to their lives. They skip school when they wish, and many of them find it impossible to make their grades. They cannot make their way in modern society, they cannot hold jobs, and in later life they have great difficulty in raising their families. As teenagers and young adults there is nothing for them to do but hang around the reserve without supervision and get into trouble. Those who do make their grades and get ahead are often made to feel the effort is futile because there is no reward for them at the end of the road. Many young people find themselves before the court. Their parents often do not attend court with their children even when the court worker has explained to them that they should be there.

Children involved in court for breaking into the school, stealing from the store or a gas shed are often sniffers who were looking for something to sniff, and their probation reports often say the parents are drinkers who spend a lot of money on booze. I find it very peculiar, but the information from the police is sometimes that parents are so involved in religion that they do not have time to spend in giving guidance to their young people. It is regrettable that the heavy drinkers and the Born Again Christians have this in common—frequently they are doing something else on the warm summer nights while the children and young people are getting into serious mischief. Parents like this are not available to give proper guidance to their children. When the chief or a judge of the court tells them to take responsibility for their children they do not listen.

By the time the children are teenagers they see themselves as people about whom no one cares. By the time they are young adults they have lost hope of a better life. The children of the drinkers eventually become like their parents, and in turn they pass their negative characteristics along to the next generation, and their children will in turn have no sense that the bosom of their community is a safe and satisfying place to be.

We all know that the bureaucratic system has not always dealt intelligently or honorably with the Indians of Canada. In recent years, however, an effort has been made to improve the lives of the Aboriginal people, and I point to better schools, Native policing, excellent health services, airstrips, roads, radio and television, and many other changes. It is up to the people themselves to take advantage of the good things and reject the bad things offered by the larger society.

It is also up to the people to be sure their children learn about the beautiful and wonderful things to be found in their own heritage. I am thinking about the quiet and loving family life that once existed at Atikwa Bay and elsewhere, and still exists in many Indian communities. I am thinking about the Indian way of sharing property and joys and sorrows between friends and neighbours. I am thinking about the ideal of respect for others, which was once so important in Indian culture. Respect for other people, respect for other points of view, and respect for the environment and all its creatures. Perhaps most of all I am thinking about respect for the notion that there is a Supreme Being whose laws must be obeyed, which is another way of saying we must respect our fellow man and our own selves.

The lessons of sharing and respect are ones the whole world could learn from the Indian people. I truly believe that the Creator has placed an obligation on the Indian people to teach these things to the rest of the world. There are leaders among you who could show you how to do this, if they would, and if you would listen to them.

By all means hang on to the finer aspects of your culture and traditions, for they are what distinguishes you from other races. Put aside the bad influences that come to you from the larger society. I know, it is stupid and wicked of non-aboriginal people to bombard you with certain influences, but in this complicated world it is sometimes difficult to tell what is good and what is bad, or to predict what the end result of an action will be. Besides, we cannot simply yank back the harm that has been done. You must find the strength and the wisdom to recognize good and evil, and make choices about how you want to live your lives. When well-meaning outsiders of any racial background try to tell you all your traditions are bad, or all the ways of non-aboriginal society are bad you must have the fortitude to reject what they say. You must think for yourselves.

Don't spend too much time thinking on how terrible it is that the white man took away your way of life. He has been doing this sort of thing for thousands of years in Europe and elsewhere. Making war on a large scale is not one of the nicer traits of the people of this world, but it seems that all races have been doing it to each other since the dawn of time. One must remember that if Columbus had not come to America in 1492 and brought all those changes with him, sooner or later it would have been someone else. We can't roll history back.

The point is, what has been done is done, and it would be more profitable to look ahead to what can be done to improve the lives of your children rather than spending time looking back on your grievances. Put behind you the bad influences of non-aboriginal society, and while you are at it don't be too proud to re-examine your own culture and traditions for counter-productive or obsolete practices that do not contribute to a good life.

What I am suggesting here is that you should deliberately reject some of your old traditions along with those influences of white society you consider to be bad. I am suggesting nothing less than that you should bring forth a whole new set of values for yourselves, a set that takes into account those beautiful old traditions mentioned above as well as the realities of the modern world.

Some of what we hear referred to, as "traditional values," or "culture," is probably not traditional or cultural at all, and to call them such is simply a convenient way of excusing bad behaviour. I am thinking of the cultural ethic of letting children do as they wish without supervision. I am thinking of the tendency to relegate women to a second-class position, or worse. I am thinking of the practice which exists at Atikwa Bay and elsewhere of allowing young girls to be "broken in" by a group of teenage boys, and then excusing it by saying, "Well that's the way it happens, you know. There's not much can be done about it."

So often when the police investigate a case of sexual abuse or family violence I hear someone who purports to be speaking for the Indian people (perhaps even a lawyer) say, "Butt out. You are interfering in a traditional behaviour pattern that is part of Native culture, and it is none of your business." I think to myself that this is nonsense. If such behaviour is traditional, then it is an aspect of Native culture that should be put away in a dark and shameful corner.

It seems if someone with white hair says that something is traditional, or cultural, then no one dares to say anything different. You know very well that the elders are not always right about what they say is traditional any more than the preachers, the judges and the teachers from the non-aboriginal world are always right. White people, particularly government people, shrink from being critical of the elders for fear of giving insult. This is a polite thing to do, but it does not advance the cause of Truth. I say that the Native people themselves should decide what is truly the Indian way, and speak up loud and clear to deny those things that do not fit with the good image of Native culture. In examining true Native culture you may lose your way in the swamp, and then you may wish to have regard to traditions as an inspiration. But when a tradition is clearly counter-productive to a better life it should be ignored no matter what the white-haired people of any race have to say about it.

Now, I hope you won't say that the non-aboriginal society is again forcing changes on you. Change seems to be what this world is about, and all of us — Indian, White, Black and Asian — are faced with it constantly. We either evolve, and adapt to it, or we perish like the dinosaurs. Change is not something that afflicts only the Indian people of North America, and we are all together on a roller-coaster ride. We must accept that some change is inevitable. In examining your values and modifying your lifestyle do not forget to have regard to both your traditional elders and to young people who have an education. But in the end you must make up your own minds about what is good and bad, and accept only the good things from both worlds.

I now come to the most difficult part of what I have to say, in which, if I am to speak truthfully as I promised in the beginning, I must be openly critical of what I perceive to be certain unprofitable aspects of Indian culture. I assure you that my aim is only to help you think your way through to changes in the way you live, which will lead to a satisfying life for your children. I know that my criticisms do not apply to all Native people, and if you are someone to whom my criticisms do not apply, then please hear me out with good grace. Perhaps you might even be moved to take my side in any discussions about this letter.

What follows can really be condensed down to two proposals:1) The Anicinabe of Atikwa Bay should take more responsibility for themselves and their families by showing genuine leadership, and continuing to do so even when the children are older, perhaps even after they have left home; and, 2) The Anicinabe of Atikwa Bay should return to their ancestral way of respecting themselves and others.

The following behaviour patterns, all of which are related to some degree, must be changed. They must not be justified by being said to be Indian things to do.

Drinking to Excess and Sniffing

These activities are certainly not Indian traditions, and they are nothing to be proud of. The people of Atikwa Bay know far better than I the harm they do, particularly to young people. No one but the individual drunk or sniffer can decide he doesn't want to do it any more. Is it worth it to continue with the drinking lifestyle when it so clearly weakens your race and contributes to the unhappiness and deaths of your children? I say to the drinkers, don't put your heads in the sand and pretend that you are not part of the problem. You are the problem.

Family Violence

Statistics gathered by the Native Women's Association show that many Native men are violent to their women folk on occasion. This also happens in other races, and I don't want to sound preachy about it, but I am sorry to say that in Atikwa Bay it is at an extreme level.

Even if someone could show me that family violence is a traditional thing, or "cultural," I would still say that it has to stop. If it is cultural, then it is nevertheless a bad thing, and is counter-productive to the well-being of those who are exposed to it. It breeds an atmosphere in which no family member can feel comfortable. It causes young people to despair and to want to be somewhere else. The boys in the family will grow up to beat their wives, because that is what their fathers did. The girls will accept it just as their mothers did. The cycle of bitterness will continue, and somewhere down the road a young person will feel discouraged because he sees no hope of a better life ahead. Do I have to remind you of the recent terrible suicides that have afflicted your people because of drinking and violence?

Sexual Abuse of Children and Women

This activity is particularly evil, but it goes on in many communities. I have heard that it started in residential schools when venal priests and teachers did unspeakable things to children. But then I have heard that the practice has always been present among the people of Northern Canada. I do not know where the truth lies. Whatever its origins, it is a dreadful, appalling thing, and it must be stopped, just as the abuse of women must be stopped.

What is most shameful is that the elders, and even whole communities, often come to the aid of an offender by covering up for him. I have personally observed that often the people will pretend that such a thing never happened, or they may say that the child or young woman is to blame. They may ask the law to turn a blind eye to the event, promising that the elders will handle it in a traditional way, but in fact the elders will not deal with the matter unless it is to sweep it under the carpet. One often finds that the senior people on the reserve do all they can to prevent the guilty party (if he is a man) from coming to trial. I have seen this evil force at work in many villages, and I say that it is a force that weakens the race. It is a vicious and degrading practice forced upon the weaker members of the society who find themselves with no one to turn to in the community for safety, not even their own relatives, who may be the worst offenders.

One does not need the advice of mental health professionals to understand that children growing up in an atmosphere of sexual abuse and hypocrisy will feel that they are worthless creatures who do not deserve the protection of their families, their clans, and their people. We have seen the sad results of such despair.

Think about these things before you try to justify sexual abuse by saying, "Well, it's common, you know. We look after that sort of thing ourselves. We do not like to hang out our dirty laundry for all to see." I have yet to hear of a case in Northern Ontario where a band council, or elders, or a justice committee looked after a sexual abuse problem themselves, except to cover it up. I know of many, many cases where the children went on to have serious problems later in life. I know of no case where a society that did not trouble to protect its women and children ever grew into a strong race.

Non-interference in the Lives of Children

There is a contradiction in the attitude of many First Nations people towards the education of your young people. On the one hand your leaders want more and better schools for the young people. On the other hand, there are those people (may we call them traditional people?) who do not insist that their children go to school. I understand from my Native associates that in the traditional world adults cease to exercise direct influence in the lives of children at an early age, and this of type child raising is still quite common even in families that are exposed to modern ways. Traditional families may not, for example, require their children to come home at an early hour in the evening. In the summer the children may be allowed to stay out all night. Often children are not required to go to school if they do not wish to.

No doubt this way of rearing children was quite suitable in days gone by when the responsibility for raising children was shared by large family groups and even by whole villages. The children could come and go as they pleased, and could play at games which prepared them to be adults. They did not have to get up early to go to school, as there was no school. They learned by watching older people. The only discipline was the approval or disapproval of the group, and it likely only consisted of ridiculing any child that offended against group standards.

But times change. Today a child, any child, must know much more than he can learn just by observing his parents, if he is to acquire the foundation of a satisfying life. This calls for continued encouragement and direction in the lives of young people. Parents should be careful to give their children guidance and support as long as they need it, and not cast them adrift too soon.

No one enjoys forcing a child to do something he does not want to do. In this regard I use the word "discipline," which is a term that can be misunderstood. It does not necessarily mean spanking a child, it merely means laying down rules and exercising firm control when the situation calls for it. It is my view that all parents of all races have a duty to exercise control over their children by requiring them to meet certain standards of behaviour. Setting a good example and offering loving discipline are usually enough to ensure success. To do anything less is to set the children up for failure in life.

Think about how you are dealing with the young people in your family. If they are not doing well is it perhaps because you are not giving them the discipline and loving guidance they need? Perhaps you are following the old tradition, or cultural ethic, of non-interference in the lives of other people, in this case your own children. Perhaps it is no longer a useful tradition, at least not in child rearing, and you should abandon it. If you do not think the school is teaching your child properly, the remedy is not to let the child skip school, but to go to the teacher, or the principal, or the parents group, and tell them about it. If there are certain skills, customs or attitudes which are important to you and would be of value to your children which the schools are not teaching them, teach them those things yourself. Schools are educational facilities equipped to deal primarily with academic subjects; it is not intended or even desirable that they provide training in personal lifestyle, religious or behavioral attitudes, which a child should learn from the family and thereby acquire a strong personal sense of values, which will guide the child through to adulthood. Are the families of Atikwa Bay able to provide their children with a good set of values? I think they can, but many families are failing miserably in this respect, and their young people are the sad products of this failure.

The Tendency to Avoid Taking Responsibility

This is another way of behaving, which does not belong exclusively to the Indian people, and it causes mischief whenever it crops up. I include it here because it seems to me to be particularly harmful to attaining a better life at Atikwa Bay and elsewhere in the North. It is closely related to the non-interference ethic which I discussed earlier, and shows up whenever a person trys to evade responsibility for doing something, or omitting to do something, which it is his duty to do, for example failing to require your children to attend school.

It comes all too easily to most of us to let someone else do a job that is really our responsibility, if we can find someone who is damn fool enough to do it. The larger society has neglected its First Nations people for so long that it now has a sense of guilt, and has spent the last thirty or so years bending over backwards to make things right. Perhaps the Anicinabek have gone too far in allowing non-aboriginal people to take responsibility for some of the things they should have been doing for themselves.

Admittedly, I am an outsider looking in, and my understanding is imperfect, but this is what I see.

Firstly, there is the matter of the rearing of children, previously discussed. It appears to me that many people who raise their children in the so-called traditional way, by allowing them to do pretty much as they please, are really just evading their responsibilities in this new age. You might wish to think very carefully about the proper role of parents in giving guidance to children and young adults. You may also wish to encourage your elders to have more contact with your children.

The Jewish people have a saying you might appropriately consider here. It is "Show me a successful child and I'll show you a pushy mother." It means simply that if a child gets along well in life the chances are that there is a strong guiding influence behind him. I have seldom seen a young person in trouble at school or before the courts that had strong and responsible parents. There may be a lesson here about unhappy young people who do away with themselves.

Secondly, the other side of the coin is that there is a tendency to put the responsibility for raising children off on the schools. Many people avoid the responsibility altogether of making their children go to school, but when they do go the parents expect the school to take on the job of raising them. Even matters of family life are left to the teachers. The teachers supervise bath night. The teachers prepare the ball diamonds, the hockey rinks, and the school concerts. Only occasionally does a parent or older person come forward to help. If a child does damage to a school, even very serious damage, the parents often take the attitude that the problem is between the child and the school authorities. Some parents will not even stand with their children in court unless a police officer makes them do it. This attitude passes a message to the child that the parent really does not care, thereby adding to the child's despair.

A third way of avoiding responsibility, one which I believe just might apply to the whole reserve, is to dump it on the police. Take the matter of children sniffing, for example. The responsibility for stopping children from sniffing starts with the parents, not with the chief and council, and certainly not with the police. Parents who do not know (or care!) where their children are, or what they are doing, are not doing the right thing by their children. The police should not be expected to substitute for parents in this way. Certainly if the police find children sniffing they should take action to stop it, but it is quite impossible for a handful of police officers to follow several hundred children around day and night—the parents should be the first to take responsibility for doing this.

Similarly, it is an error to expect the police to stop everyone from drinking and bringing liquor to the reserve. Of course, the police should get tough with offenders when they catch them, but it would take hundreds of policemen to ring the reserve twenty-four hours a day to stop the flow of booze to a population that is determined to drink no matter what.

A wise man once said, "The police are the people and the people are the police." It means that the police are powerless to act in matters of social responsibility, or lifestyle, without the cooperation of the people themselves. Think about this. How can a few police officers be at the airstrip, on the waterfront or the ice road, and keeping watch on suspected houses, all at the same time? It is impossible. Besides, when you think about it, you wouldn't really want a situation where the police were everywhere in your lives, regulating and exercising control over all your activities from morning 'til night. That degree of police involvement would be an excessive intrusion of authority, which the population would have good reason to resent. Canada's government and legal structure is so designed as to make it virtually impossible to ever become a police state, as is the case in some countries in the world.

How can the police obtain convictions in court against bootleggers (or rapists or thieves or child molesters or wife beaters) if ordinary people who know the facts refuse to cooperate by telling their story in open court? The police cannot come into court and say, "Charlie Kestablish told me he saw the accused with a bottle of liquor," because that is hearsay evidence, and not acceptable. Charlie Kestablish must come to court and say it himself. If he "forgets," or simply fades away on court day, the accused will go unpunished.

What I am saying here is that if ordinary people evade their responsibility to help the police, the reserve will never become a safe and comfortable place to live. Every one of you, particularly your young people, will be the poorer for it.

If you wish to create a better life for yourselves and your children you are going to have to make a hard choice. You are either going to have to put up with bad behaviour from drinkers and law breakers, even family members, or you are going to have to make a new tradition, one of cooperation with the police and the courts and your chief. If you cannot cooperate with the very people who would make your life better for you, don't complain about the abusers and drinkers and other lawbreakers.

In closing, I want to emphasize what I said on the matter of tradition. Traditions are useful when you have lost your way and need a source of inspiration. However, they may not be of assistance in dealing with all the new problems that beset you and all members of Canadian society in this fast moving world. Think about the many fine traditions and cultural ethics that belong to your race, and hold them dear. But don't be afraid to create new traditions when the old ones have lost their usefulness.

Afterword

Ted died on March 4, 2004, after a lengthy hospital stay, due to complications following heart surgery. He chose to undergo a risky medical procedure, as he believed it was preferable to take a chance rather than submit to the inevitable progression of his illness. He completed work on this book, but did not live to see it in print.

Index

More HANCOCK HOUSE *biography titles*

Wheels, Skis and Floats
E.C. (Ted) Burton, Robert S. Grant
ISBN 0-88839-428-4
5.5 x 8.5 • sc • 176 pp.

Journal of a Country Lawyer
E.C. (Ted) Burton
ISBN 0-88839-364-4
5.5 x 8.5 • sc • 240 pp.

Afloat in Time
Jim Sirois
ISBN 0-88839-455-1
5.5 x 8.5 • sc • 288 pp.

Alaska in the Wake of the North Star
Loel Shuler
ISBN 0-88839-587-6
5.5 x 8.5 • sc • 224 pp.

Crazy Cooks & Gold Miners
Joyce Yardley
ISBN 0-88839-294-X
5.5 x 8.5 • sc • 224 pp.

Dead Man's Clothes
Dale Davidson
ISBN 978-0-88839-608-2
5.5 x 8.5 • sc • 144 pp.

A Doctor's Notes
T.F. Godwin
ISBN 978-0-88839-654-9
5.5 x 8.5 • sc • 368 pp.

Loggers of the BC Coast
Hans Knapp
ISBN 0-88839-588-4
5.5 x 8.5 • sc • 200 pp.

Nahanni Trailhead
Joanne Ronan Moore
ISBN 0-88839-464-0
5.5 x 8.5 • sc • 256 pp.

Out of the Rain
Paul Jones
ISBN 0-88839-541-8
5.5 x 8.5 • sc • 272 pp.

Outposts & Bushplanes
Bruce Lamb
ISBN 0-88839-556-6
5.5 x 8.5 • sc • 208 pp.

Ralph Edwards of Lonesome Lake
Ed Gould
ISBN 0-88839-100-5
5.5 x 8.5 • sc • 296 pp.

Raven and the Mountaineer
Monty Alford
ISBN 0-88839-542-6
5.5 x 8.5 • sc • 152 pp.

Rivers of Gold
Gwen & Don Lee
ISBN 0-88839-555-8
5.5 x 8.5 • sc • 204 pp.

Ruffles on my Longjohns
Isabel Edwards
ISBN 0-88839-102-1
5.5 x 8.5 • sc • 297 pp.

Timeless Trails of the Yukon
Dolores Cline Brown
ISBN 0-88839-584-5
5.5 x 8.5 • sc • 184 pp.

Tomekichi Homma
K.T. Homma, C.G. Isaksson
ISBN 978-0-88839-660-0
5.5 x 8.5 • sc • 72 pp.

Walter Moberly and the Northwest Passage by Rail
Daphne Sleigh
ISBN 0-88839-510-8
5.5 x 8.5 • sc • 272 pp.

White Water Skippers of the North
Nancy Warren Ferrell
ISBN 978-0-88839-616-7
5.5 x 8.5 • sc • 216 pp.

Wild Roses
dutchie Rutledge-Mathison
ISBN 978-0-88839-625-9
5.5 x 8.5 • sc • 72 pp.

Yukon Tears and Laughter
Joyce Yardley
ISBN 0-88839-594-9
5.5 x 8.5 • sc • 176 pp.

hancock house

View all HANCOCK HOUSE *titles at* **www.hancockhouse.com**